MODERN CIVIL AIRCRAFT: 9

BOEING 737

B-2501

Alan J. Wright

LONDON

IAN ALLAN LTD

First published 1991

ISBN 0 7110 1955 X

Published by Ian Allan Ltd, Shepperton, Surrey; and printed by Ian Allan Printing Ltd at their works at Coombelands in Runnymede, England

Acknowledgements
Grateful thanks are extended to Boeing's Public Relations Division and its UK respresentative, Dick Kenny, for help given during the preparation of this book. Useful assistance was also given by a number of airlines, the USAF and various individuals, in particular, George W. Pennick.

Alan J. Wright

Abbreviations

AAIB	Air Accidents Investigation Branch	FAA	Federal Aviation Administration
AFB	Air Force Base	FTW	Flying Training Wing
BA	British Airways	IT	Inclusive Tour
BAC	British Aircraft Corporation	NTSB	National Transportation Safety Board
CAA	Civil Aviation Authority	SAS	Scandinavian Airlines System
CRT	Cathode Ray Tube	TEA	Trans European Airways

Air Europe was launched in 1979 with the help of 737-200 G-BMOR. *A. S. Wright*

MODERN CIVIL AIRCRAFT: 9
BOEING 737

For over 20 years the 737 in its various guises has carried countless millions on their travels, whether for business or pleasure. In the US the type has been mostly employed on scheduled services, but in Europe it has played a large part in the foreign holiday boom. There can be few people who have not travelled to the sunspots of the Mediterranean on board one of the baby Boeings at some time or other. Many would never have had the opportunity but for the ability of the tour operators to offer inclusive tour (IT) packages at extremely low prices. This was largely made possible by the operating economics of the modern airliners, particularly the 737.

Nevertheless, there has always been a price to pay. In order to keep costs at an attractive level but at the same time obtain a little profit from the activities, the airlines were obliged to fit as many seats as practical into the cabins. Strangely the leisure passengers rarely comment upon the safety aspect of the airliners' cramped interiors, preferring perhaps to ignore the subject in the interest of peace of mind. In any case the IT traveller invariably seeks the cheapest ticket available, so is prepared to suffer a degree of discomfort for a couple of hours or so.

On the other hand, businessmen are not concerned about cost, but are interested in comfort, convenience and safety. For this reason the 737s employed on schedules usually carry two-class cabins to cater for those in this category; in some case having the seats arranged in pairs either side of the aisle rather than three-by-three.

Hot-galleys are now standard features on the aircraft, thereby permitting much improved in-flight catering. Of course, whether hot or cold, the same difficulties exist when attempting to eat the meal. Although the small bag of assorted tools accompanying the contents of the tray includes a knife and fork, use of both at the same time is not particularly practical without some prearranged co-operation with the immediate neighbour. It is especially unfortunate if the occupant of the middle seat of a batch of three has failed to respond to a weight-watcher's campaign. Retrieval of any item accidentally dropped on the floor also presents some difficulties and certainly requires a reasonable level of physical fitness before attempting the necessary contortions. To some extent this may explain the amount of litter strewn beneath the seats and left by the disembarking travellers. An army of cleaners is required while the machine is being turned round; any delay being received with annoyance by the new batch of potential rubbish generators. While no one could claim that the all-tourist 737 seating arrangement offers any more than just adequate space, the speedy journey usually compensates for any temporary inconvenience. Anyway, there is often the comforting thought that some passengers have paid much more for a ticket on the same aircraft.

Despite the travel boom, the manufacturers endured several periods of sluggish sales, but towards the end of the 1980s the trend was reversed as Boeing received a record number of orders for its wares. To meet the demand, production rates at Seattle had to be increased, but not without difficulties. During 1989 there were 14 737s completed each month; a figure raised to 17 in 1990. Similar adjustments were made to the 747, 757 and 767 lines, but the general speed-up in the factory brought an acute shortage of skilled staff at all levels. This situation not only affected Boeing, but also its many suppliers, who were forced to accelerate their output so that the flow of components could be maintained.

Inevitably this led to staff dissatisfaction and a lowering of standards. After a number of wiring discrepancies were discovered in newly-delivered aircraft, tighter quality control was introduced so that Boeing could recover its reputation in the industry. Although still the world's leading manufacturer, the company has considerable competition from McDonnell Douglas and Airbus Industrie. This was clearly emphasised when it was not invited to supply a massive block of up to 239 aircraft to the closely associated European carriers, Austrian Airlines, Finnair, SAS and Swissair. Probably Boeing was not unduly surprised because the quartet have always been McDonnell Douglas supporters, but the chance to win the order would undoubtedly have been welcome.

Meanwhile the 737 is likely to remain the company's most successful jet transport as it continues well into the next century, in some cases re-engined or with the assistance of the forthcoming hush-kit designed to comply with the noise regulations.

At the end of World War 2, jet-propulsion was still very much in its infancy, yet the idea for an airliner powered by this new form of engine was already being considered in the UK by de Havilland. Originally intended as a fast mailplane, the company's design grew until it became the 36-seat Comet 1 by the time the aircraft entered commercial service on 2 May 1952, Amazingly, only 11 years had elapsed since the maiden flight of the prototype, single-seat, experimental Gloster E28/39 and its Whittle powerplant which marked the birth of the jet-age.

While the early Comets suffered tragic losses, the aircraft was by no means a failure, because it demonstrated the vast possibilities for future air travel. During its short operational life with the airlines, the Mk 1 proved that the concept was a realistic proposition, and certainly became extremely popular with the travelling public. Although the British manufacturer was the first to produce a practical airliner and was responsible for the rapid growth in interest, there were many design offices worldwide which were searching for alternative outlets for their talents now that wartime priorities had vanished.

On the other hand, in the US Boeing had continued to concentrate on the development of its B-47 jet-powered bomber in the late 1940s, because the company was not entirely convinced that the economics would be acceptable to the airline industry. However, by using this valuable experience, in the early 1950s work began on the design of a military tanker/transport, which was identified as the Model 367-80. By focusing its efforts on this machine there was every chance that an order would be forthcoming from the government, thereby helping to defray development costs. This proved to be the case in 1955, so once again the traditional benefactor brought a smile to the custodian of the company's finances.

Following this welcome injection of funds, the commercial 707 variant was offered to the airline. Pan American became the prime target and in October 1955 the carrier responded with an order for 20 of the new transports. Boeing was not alone in the quest for customers, because in California Douglas was actively marketing its own offering in the guise of the DC-8. In fact the latter was favoured by Pan Am because its slightly wider fuselage enabled a greater variety of seat configurations. Therefore 25 examples of the type were also selected as an insurance against possible problems with the delivery of the 707s.

These enormous orders from such an influential airline forced rival operators to advance their re-equipment plans in order to remain competitive. The US West Coast became the destination for management teams from the world's leading companies, but despite the huge sales penetration, both manufacturers lost money on the programme. Douglas did not have the advantage of a military contract to offset development costs amounting to hundreds of millions of dollars, inevitably making its product more expensive than the 707. This factor, plus its two-year lead advantage, enabled the latter to outsell the DC-8 and helped to elevate Boeing to the front ranks of the transport manufacturers. Twice in the past this position had been lost to Douglas so it was particularly gratifying for the company to be in the vanguard at the beginning of the jet age.

Unfortunately this had not been achieved painlessly. From an early stage, losses on the 707 had been steadily escalating, mainly due to the manufacturer's efforts to constantly incorporate a steady stream of technological advances. Consequently, during the type's first two years of existence, it was available with two different wing designs, three fuselage lengths and a similar number of engine choices. Boeing had also responded to the growing demand for a medium-range airliner by generally shrinking the 707 into the Model 720, hoping that the result would be an attractive addition to the family. In the event it won relatively limited success with production ending in 1967 after only 154 examples had been completed.

Many airlines still considered the type to be too large for domestic short-haul sectors and wanted something with between 125 and 150 seats, together with low operating costs. Research carried out in the 1950s had confirmed the fact that a large market existed for such an airliner, but how this could be achieved posed many problems, not the least being the considerable financial investment involved. Opinions differed as to whether or not Boeing should commit itself to yet another civil transport with its undoubted risks. There was significant support for a decision to concentrate resources back on to military projects, which normally enjoyed a degree of government subsidy. After much debate the company opted to persevere in the commercial market, which meant that serious studies began on the 727 even before the operational debut of the 707.

Above:
Boeing offered the 720 for use on short-to-medium range sectors with moderate success. Conair employed OY-DSP for IT charters in later years. *AJW*

Uppermost in the thoughts of the designers were the engines. While it was unanimously agreed that the presence of these devices was essential, opinions differed as to the quantity needed. Already the Caravelle had proved that two were adequate for this class of airliner, although the Viscount relied upon four turbo-props, a mode of power by no means dismissed by the manufacturer. Consultation with the major carriers did little to help. United continued to specify four engines to retain acceptable safety margins, while American Airlines was content with a couple. For good measure three were most favoured by Eastern; a total thought to be a good compromise between excellent safety margins and reduced costs. Under the circumstances it is surprising that the eager quest for economy did not bring forth a call for a single-engined variant!

Armed with this selection of opinions, Boeing's design team set about producing something suitable for the duties that the aircraft would be expected to perform. These would include the ability to operate swiftly and safely into the smaller airports and be capable of quick turn-rounds. Such activities would also demand a structure built to give a much longer fatigue life because customers could not afford to change their expensive possessions too frequently. Various configurations were considered, ranging from a scaled-down 707 to a design equipped with two aft-mounted engines. Calculations on comparative costs continued but did nothing to allay the fears of those monitoring the evap-oration of Boeing's funds. Development figures for a trijet were even more depressing, so understandably interest tended to wane, leaving a wing-mounted twin-jet as the most favoured at this point.

Unlike the pioneering days of the 707, Boeing had to contend with the presence of several other manufacturers aiming at the same market. American, Eastern, Trans World and United were already identified as possible launch customers so the design emerging from the factory had to meet their needs so far as possible. Over 150 possible solutions were studied to determine the most efficient layout for the wing and fuselage. It was essential that the new machine should be capable of fast point-to-point flights, but at the same time able to land at low speeds on fairly short runways. This feature was stipulated by Eastern because of its extensive use of New York's La Guardia airport and its restrictive 4,860ft runway. For this reason the airline was a strong supporter of a twin or trijet. United certainly was not. In this case the carrier needed something with power for operations from the hot and high situations at its Denver hub. Four engines were therefore considered essential.

To achieve these difficult objectives, Boeing designed special triple-slotted trailing-edge flaps, together with an assortment of similar control surfaces on the wing's leading edge. They provided the aircraft with 25% more wing area when fully extended, which in turn permitted low landing speeds. Flight testing of the devices lasted almost a year, and was carried out by the busy Dash Eighty now that it had completed its 707 work. It also acquired an additional engine nacelle on the rear fuselage so that the effects of this arrangement could be analysed. Results

Above:
When the 737 was being developed, the cheaper turboprop Electra was still a competitor. Air Florida operated three on its interstate flights, one being N24AF. *Sherlock via G. W. Pennick*

confirmed that the proposal to group a trijet's powerplant at the rear of the fuselage was completely feasible in conjunction with a T-tail.

Eventually the design team produced three alternative layouts for either two, three or four engines, the final decision depending upon the sales success. By the time that the company's board finally gave a cautious go-ahead in February 1960, two of the likely customers had been lost. American had chosen the much cheaper and already available Lockheed Electra turboprop while TWA was no longer in a position to spend any money. Although there was every confidence in the 727, Boeing was still somewhat reluctant to make a large investment in the project without the comfort of some firm orders. Accordingly a target of 100 commitments was set for the sales department to achieve before the deadline of 1 December, otherwise the whole scheme would be stillborn.

With barely nine months for persuasive talks, some intensive campaigns were quickly instigated around the various airlines' offices. Naturally both United and Eastern received particular attention in the hope that one or both would launch the new generation airliner. Fortunately both carriers were prepared to compromise after detailed evaluation of the 727 on offer, each declaring its intention to order 40 of the trijet

variant. Following this welcome news, the cloud of gloom which had settled over Seattle suddenly lifted as construction of the prototype was authorised.

Almost two years later the first machine was rolled out at Renton, making its maiden trip aloft on 9 February 1963, rather later than had originally been planned. It was quickly followed by another three specimens, which enabled the test programme to proceed apace for certification before the end of the year. Both launch customers were able to begin commercial services in early February 1964 and it was not long before the two carriers found that the operating economics were better than forecast. Because the 727's very existence had largely depended upon the requirements of Eastern and United, the Series 100 was tailor-made for the purpose. This was reflected by the order book, which following the initial batch, did not record any spectacular successes. Therefore at the time that the type began its service career, the total figure had still to pass the 200 mark.

At the start of the 727 programme, Boeing had based its sums on the expectation of selling a total of 350 in a six-year period, a landmark still some distance ahead. While not too dissatisfied with progress, the manufacturer introduced two variants of the Series 100 designed to appeal to a wider market. First came the C version, which was readily convertible from passenger to cargo layout. For this purpose the species was given a large loading door in the port side forward fuselage, together with a strengthened cabin

floor. As in the standard model, a total of 94 seats could be carried, but this figure could be varied by means of a movable bulkhead. As an alternative, customers were also given the option of a quick-change (QC) variant, the transformation from passenger to cargo mode being possible in one hour.

While the new offerings received support, Boeing recognised that an upsurge in traffic generally indicated that a larger model was now likely to succeed. Known as the Series 200, the developed 727 was given a fuselage stretched by 20ft (3.05m) and a capacity for 189 seats. In other respects there was little difference between the two versions, so inevitably the performance of the 200 suffered somewhat. This disadvantage was rectified in the early 1970s when the manufacturer introduced the Advanced model which incorporated more powerful engines, increased fuel tankage and a range of other improvements designed to enhance the aircraft's overall efficiency and economics.

Throughout the period, the 727 had been sold steadily, but the latest model ensured even greater success. On several occasions during the 1960s and 1970s the turbulent nature of the aircraft industry brought troubled times to many companies, but Boeing was supported by the 727 and its profitability. Eventually 1,832 examples were built to give it the distinction of becoming the world's best-selling jet airliner. Production ended in August 1984 as it became over-shadowed by the advanced new generation types: the twin-engined 757 and 767.

Back in the 1950s this was, of course, Boeing's preferred configuration for its short/medium range design, but at the time circumstances dictated that a trijet would be more likely to be accepted by the airline industry. From experience with the 707 and 727 the manufacturer had learned that to maintain a hold on the market it was necessary to develop models that appealed to a wide range of customers, rather than to concentrate on the requirements of one individual carrier. No doubt Boeing observed the fate of the early Trident which suffered irreparable damage to its prospects by trying to meet the ever-changing specifications issued by British European Airways. With this in mind and the 727 established, attention was turned towards a truly short range transport.

Understandably there was a greater air of confidence at the Seattle plant when the design team began preliminary work on what had already been designated the Model 737. During 1964 there were scant details released, but from those which did percolate through the security screen it could be gleaned that the latest project was intended to carry between 50 and 60 passengers on routes ranging from 50 to 1,000 miles in length. Once again the aircraft was to offer the minimum direct operating costs and be capable of earning a profit even with 35% load factors.

With the basic outline design completed, Boeing despatched its sales personnel off to seek the opinions of a wide variety of carriers in assorted countries. From these visits the company was gratified to receive a favourable response from the airlines, many of those approached expressing the view that the One-Eleven and DC-9 alternatives were too large for their present needs. It was therefore surprising that when the indefatigable sales team descended upon the Australian domestic operators, the 737 version on offer had quietly grown to an 80-seater. Previously there had been keen interest in the smaller capacity machine, but the revised proposals did not meet with quite the same enthusiasm.

As 1964 moved into its last quarter, Boeing was still unwilling to disclose any detailed information on its latest member of the family, pending a decision on a go-ahead. However, some aspects of the design philosophy were forthcoming, the most significant indicating that there would be a return to wing-mounted engines. This conclusion was reached after lengthy investigations into the most advantageous position for the powerplant when taking performance and economics into account. Some of the factors considered during the comparison exercise were the degree of wing sweep-back and chord, the distance of the engine pod from the fuselage, size of fin and the stall effects created by the necessary T-tail associated with side-located engines.

By moving a pylon-mounted engine further inboard on a sharply-swept wing, the resulting change in the position of the centre of gravity (C of G) required the rear fuselage to be length-ened to compensate. When using a side-mounted powerplant any fuselage balancing adjustments had to be made towards the nose. Although this is the traditional location for the flightdeck, there were no suggestions made that perhaps the employment of crew endowed with above average proportions would be useful. Nacelle sizes had also grown since the idea of moving the engines to the rear had become fashionable, making the practice more difficult for the designers. With a chord small enough in relation to the engine, then it was possible to achieve a favourable underwing position without loss of performance.

Modern jets were quite capable of flying with one engine shut down, but the effects of asymmetric thrust had to be considered. With the advent of the fuselage-mounted powerplants the problem had become almost non-existent, but in the case of underwing arrangement the matter came to the fore once again. To counter any tendency for the aircraft to deviate from its intended track, a larger fin was deemed necessary, although this in turn brought the handicap of extra weight. There were obviously advantages and disadvantages in both configurations but Boeing calculated that with the engines under the wing at least 1,500lb could be saved. Capacity was also improved because with the turbines attached to the side of the fuselage, there was always an area between them which could not be used for seats. Instead it was frequently utilised for items of upperdeck cargo or toilet accommodation, although the space available usually exceeded that needed for the latter. At least it was possible to actually turn round in the confines of the compartment and lengthy occupation was discouraged by the noise from the adjacent jets. Now this seemed likely to end.

Ever since the birth of the jet, the inviting hole at the front of the powerplant has proved fascinating for any adventurous foreign object. With underwing engine intakes close to the ground, it was expected that their move further aft on the 727 would all but eliminate the danger. Research carried out by Boeing revealed that there were basically three different types of ingestion. Not surprisingly it was not unknown for a loose pebble to be flicked into the nearby aperture by the nose wheel, but statistics proved that these missiles were also despatched with equal regularity into the unsuspecting cavity at the rear. There was also the distinct possibility of more damage following reverse thrust application so it was concluded that neither layout possessed any significant advantages.

One of the major selling points for the rear-engined airliner had always been the quieter cabin. This claim was certainly true during take-off and the initial climb but beyond this point, once again there was little difference. Much of the noise generated was aerodynamic in origin and since a short-haul type was expected to fly high speed sectors at lower altitude, this source would be even more audible.

Other features taken into account by Boeing during its prolonged deliberations were the accessibility of the cargo compartment and the ease by which routine engine maintenance could be carried out. Standing on the ground is always preferable to the use of steps and platforms, so given the choice the engineers consulted favoured the wing engine. Freight loaders were divided in their opinions, but really the position of the powerplant had little detrimental effect on their territory.

At the start of 1965 there had still been no firm announcement from Seattle concerning the prospects of the 737. This silence was taken to indicate that the manufacturer was near to receiving letters of intent for enough aircraft to justify production. Finally on 19 February the long-awaited confirmation came when Boeing formally gave the go-ahead to its new short-range, twin turbofan transport following successful negotiations with Lufthansa. An historic occasion indeed, because the German flag carrier had become the first foreign company to launch an airliner of US design.

Below:
Baggage loading into the underfloor holds is assisted by the relatively low level of the doors, seen here open in readiness on the Aer Lingus Series 200 EI-ASH.
AJW

When Boeing first sought the views of the airline industry on the subject of a short-haul jet airliner, between 50 and 65 seats seemed to be a reasonable capacity for something in this class. However, while the possible customers were being canvassed it became plain that in the view of the majority there was a definite need for larger machines, especially with the upsurge in traffic currently underway. As a result, at the launch ceremony it was a 100 seater which was unveiled to take its place alongside the DC-9 and One-Eleven. The latter pair were already well established in production, with the former only a week from its first flight and the UK machine about to enter airline service with British United, so Boeing's entry into the same market seemed somewhat belated.

Needless to say, there were good reasons for the apparent cautiousness on the part of the US manufacturer; in part due to the development of the 727 and later variants of the 707 conspiring to keep the relevant teams fully occupied. From the start there was considerable support from within the company for the design to utilise as many 727 components and systems as possible. At the time of the preliminary studies for the latter, a good deal of work had been completed which had a direct bearing on the new project and could easily be adapted. Not only would this bring consider-able savings in time and money, but also make the end product a particularly attractive prop-osition for existing 707/727 operators. It was an opportunity that the designers could not afford to ignore, especially since the indications were that the market would support such a machine anyway. So the 737 emerged with the same cabin width as its two relatives and capable of six-abreast seating.

As usual there had been a concerted effort to attract a large order to justify the launch, much time being directed at selling the machine to United and/or Eastern. By chance the pair had been the first in the queue for the 727, so it was thought that the commonality between the types would guarantee success. However, both com-panies were still busily engaged in the evaluation of the short-haul jets on offer at the time, so in this case the distinction for ensuring that the 737 became a reality fell to Lufthansa. It was only during the last few weeks of negotiations with the German flag carrier that Boeing had bowed to a request to further expand the capacity of the airliner to accommodate 100 seats instead of 86.

Below:
The 737-100 D-ABEL was the seventh of the type to be delivered to Lufthansa in April 1968. In this photograph it has acquired the later, longer engine nacelles. *G. W. Pennick*

This growth also meant a general increase in dimensions to compensate for the changes and so the Series 100 was born.

Long before Boeing began its detailed talks with Lufthansa it had been common knowledge that the airline would soon need a replacement for its ageing piston-engined fleet. Both Douglas and the British Aircraft Corporation (BAC) sent sales teams to promote their respective campaigns and up until the last few months it appeared as though the US company would be the victor. Needless to say the news of the order came as a disappointment for BAC because it had high hopes for the One-Eleven's chances. Rumours were rife about the part played by the politicians in the affair which included the suggestion that the German government was under some pressure to force its national airline to select the British aircraft. Fortunately Lufthansa was left to make its own decision, which was certainly influenced by the fact that it already possessed both 707s and 727s. In a statement issued to coincide with the announcement of the order for 21 aircraft, the carrier stressed that the choice would bring an unusual degree of standardisation. Also unique was the fact that a foreign company had become the launch customer for a US airliner.

Such was the eagerness to win orders that all the manufacturers were willing to try to meet individual requirements if the prize was large enough. In the case of Eastern and United, neither felt that the competing designs (DC-9, One-Eleven and 737) completely met their particular needs, but both Boeing and Douglas quickly offered to develop a stretched version of their wares. The effort was well worthwhile because Eastern chose the lengthened DC-9 and Boeing won its second customer for the 737 on 5 April 1965 when United signed up for 40 examples of the projected long-bodied variant, to be identified as the Series 200. So with only two customers and the first flight still a year distant, the company was already committed to the production of two different models.

Unfortunately this availability of choice relegated the One-Eleven into third place because BAC had yet to launch a larger version in response to the growing demand. In fact it was not until British European expressed an interest that the design for the new Series 500 was finalised, resulting in the prototype's first flight on 30 June 1967 and service entry with BEA on 17 November 1968. Despite the One-Eleven's early successes across the Atlantic, the larger capacity model failed to make any impact in North America, where the sales were shared between Douglas and Boeing.

Generally the main difference between the two 737 models lay in the length of the fuselage, which was stretched by 6ft (1.82m) in the case of the 200 to increase the capacity within the cabin to 115 passengers. When comfort was of little importance, 15 extra seats could be squeezed in for all-tourist work without any alterations to the normal facilities. As this version was developed,

Below:
Originally operated by Singapore Airlines, this Series 100 later served with Air Florida as N40AF. *AJW*

aerodynamics that were intended to give maximum efficiency; an essential ingredient if Boeing was to compete successfully with Douglas and BAC. Certainly the company had a good start because of its invaluable experiences with high-lift wing development on the 707/727 series. Because the new type was intended primarily for short-haul work, high cruising speeds were of less importance than on the earlier machines. A thicker wing section was therefore possible, while the sweepback was 25° compared with 35° on the 707.

Basically the size of the wing needed to be as small as possible if minimum direct operating costs were to be obtained. In practice the area necessary was to some extent determined by the space needed to hold sufficient fuel for the specified range. In order to achieve the required performance, both leading and trailing edges were provided with an abundance of devices for assisting landings and take-offs from relatively short strips. Between the fuselage and engines a two-position Krueger flap was installed on the leading edge of the wing, while the outboard section was equipped with a three-position slat. Triple-slotted flaps accounted for some 74% of the trailing edge, extending from the fuselage to the conventional ailerons. There was no necessity to provide another pair of the latter for high-speed control as in the case of the 707/727, but the wing upper surface followed the current trend by carrying spoilers and lift dumpers in front of the trailing edge flaps.

Unlike the 707, Boeing mounted the 737's engines close to the wing's under-surface, which helped to keep the undercarriage as short as possible. Both main legs retracted sideways into the centre-fuselage wells so that the wheels created a seal, thereby eliminating the need for doors. Convention was followed for the nose-wheel unit which was designed to hinge forwards.

When the 737 was first mooted, the proposed powerplant was the Pratt & Whitney JT8D-1 turbofan of 14,000lb (6,350kg) thrust. This two-shaft engine was a front-fan derivative of the military J52 and civil JT8B series developed originally for the 727. At an early stage in the design of the twin-jet the similarly rated JT8D-7 was substituted, a change which further increased the commonality with its larger relative because the trijet was by now also equipped with this version. Hinged cowlings on the 737's two units gave easy access for maintenance purposes, and the thrust reversers fitted were the same clamshell type carried by the 727. An auxiliary power unit (APU) was installed at the rear of the fuselage for the supply of air and electrical power both in flight and on the ground,

Above:
In appearance the 737 was a fairly conventional design. Olympic was the 60th customer for the type, SX-BCA being the first to be delivered to the airline in 1976. *Boeing*

so many of the changes were incorporated into the Series 100. For instance, by moving the rear bulkhead the maximum number of seats was raised to 103, while early in the design stage the size of the vertical and horizontal tail was increased. Once the location of the engines had been established there was no advantage in using a T-tail, so an orthodox unit was proposed.

At this point, the wing-span had been set at 93ft (28.3m), a slight increase over that originally planned, but at the same time the maximum weight of both versions had increased significantly to 97,000lb (42,410kg). Meanwhile the comparable DC-9 had reached 108,000lb (48,988kg) to give the type a small payload advantage over the Boeing offering, although the long-range version of the 737-100 could carry a full load over 1,830 miles (2,945km). At least that was the confident opinion of those in charge of the company's calculators, but of course the aircraft still had to prove itself in flight.

In appearance the 737 was a fairly conventional design, but this belied the extremely advanced

Left:
Arkia's 4X-BAA shows off its flaps and slots when in a landing configuration. *G. W. Pennick*

Centre left:
There is not a lot of ground clearance for the 737's engines but it does give easier access for maintenance purposes. This Pacific Southwest example (N379PS) still had the original short nacelles in 1969.
G. W. Pennick

Below:
Peering into jet engines is popular with curious visitors, but engineers have a serious reason for the practice during the turnround of a 737. *AJW*

where engine starting was another of its allocated tasks.

One of the features of the 727 not included in the smaller machine's specification was the door and associated stairway under the rear fuselage, but passenger entry doors were provided at each end of the cabin instead. Either or both were equipped with airstairs, depending upon the specific model and customer's wishes. The layout of the 737's interior accommodation varied, but many of the items such as seats and galleys were interchangeable with those of the trijet, which was an additional bonus for operators of both types.

Another significant difference concerned the flight deck. Whereas the 727 was flown by a three-person crew, the later type was designed for two pilots from the outset. This step was readily accepted by the airlines as a further means of reducing costs, but the demise of the flight engineer caused considerable disturbances amongst the world's staff associations. For many years United was forced to fly its 737s with three cockpit crew members, but agreement was finally reached in 1981 for the company to fall into line with almost every other operator. This period of world-wide agreement did not last for very long. In Europe, Air France had been trying to order 737s for its regional services for several years, but staff opposition always prevented the move. In the autumn of 1981 a more reasonable attitude was adopted by one of the two groups representing the pilots and engineers. Encour-

Left:
Although designed with as much commonality as possible with the 727, the 737 was not given the rear, underside entrance shown in use by N4618 of Pan Am. *AJW*

Below:
The flightdeck on all the 737 models is laid out for a two-person crew. *Boeing*

aged by this change of heart, the airline placed an order for 12 of the 737-200s to become the 108th customer for the type. Further bitter battles and strikes lay ahead, but as is usually the case, common sense finally prevailed.

Needless to say, Boeing began to expand its latest family at an early stage to cater for the varying customer requirements. A mixed traffic version known as the 737C was introduced in both body lengths, but due to lack of interest no Series 100Cs were built. On the other hand the -200C was more successful with the first of its kind flying in September 1968 prior to delivery to Wien Consolidated a month later. For this combi configuration, the 737 acquired a 134in×87in (3.4m×2.2m) cargo door in the port side, forward fuselage. This allowed the aircraft's strengthened floor to carry the same size freight pallets as the 707 and 727, thereby enabling easy transfers to be made between the three types.

Converting the 737 from one role to another took a couple of hours or so, but for those wanting a faster turnround Boeing also offered the Quick Change (QC) variant. Basically it possessed the same features as the Model C, but in this case the passenger seats were mounted on pallets to facilitate a swift transformation. It was claimed that a team of six could complete the conversion in about 20min, no doubt depending upon the enthusiasm of the individuals. Even assuming the claim to be somewhat optimistic, the idea was original and laid the foundations for greater utilisation of the machine by carrying passengers during the day and freight at night.

By April 1966, one year or so after Boeing had decided to go ahead with the short-haul 737, considerable progress had been made towards bringing the newcomer to fruition. Most of the basic design engineering has been completed, and major parts of the aircraft's anatomy were steadily taking shape at the Seattle plant. Already more than 2.5 million man-hours had been spent on the project, and a vast number of parts had been issued to the workshops. Amongst the portions already completed were the centre section and stub wing for the first aircraft, which was due to be rolled out before the end of the year. At least now there was even more incentive because since the initial Lufthansa order, nine other airlines had followed suit to bring the total commitments to 96.

Sure enough, Boeing was able to complete the prototype on schedule for it to emerge from its hangar in December. Meanwhile Lufthansa's first machine (D-ABEA) was not far from completion in the assembly building, with only its various control surfaces outstanding as the time drew near for the type's aerial baptism. In the event this did not take place until 9 April 1967 when the Series 100, N73700, began its flight trials.

These proceeded according to plan, with the FAA type certificate duly awarded on 15 December, thereby meeting the target set two and a half years earlier when the project was launched. Unfortunately this impressive timetable did not extend to the deliveries. Originally Lufthansa planned to have its first machine in service before the end of 1967, but Boeing was forced to admit that unforeseen production difficulties would mean that delays of up to three months would be experienced by early customers.

Certain technical shortcomings had manifested themselves, although the manufacturer was confident that the problems could be overcome simply and swiftly. A fairly high cruising drag was experienced with the aircraft, which meant higher permitted operating weights if the payload/range guarantees were to be met. During the static testing of the airframe, parts of the rear wing spar buckled when subjected to loads 34% above those expected in flight. Although the failure occurred almost at the end of the test cycle, it naturally became necessary to strengthen the components and repeat the programme.

The two machines earmarked for the certification work were quickly modified with reinforcing to withstand up to 50% overloads, while the remaining four completed airframes received similar attention during the course of their regular maintenance. Subsequently the modifications were incorporated on the line. The higher weight also threatened some airfield performance promises despite the undoubted effectiveness of the very advanced high-lift slats and flaps. Boeing therefore set about the further development of these devices so that even more benefits could be derived.

As forecast by the manufacturer, the remedial actions were achieved without any undue problems, allowing the German pioneer to take delivery of its first 737 in December. With others quickly following, the type was able to enter service only two months or so later than intended. By the end of April 1968 — one year after the maiden flight — Boeing was in a position to announce a number of higher permissible landing weight options applicable to both Series 100 and 200 versions. The new limits allowed the aircraft to be flown over longer sectors without the need to refuel.

A short time later news was released that an improved reverse thrust unit had been designed jointly by Boeing and Rohr. During trials using the appropriately equipped prototype, the aircraft demonstrated its ability to end its landing run after only 3,000ft of the concrete strip had been covered. This impressive performance was achieved at the maximum landing weight of 95,000lb (43,100kg) and without the use of wheel brakes. Immediately it brought the prospect of greater safety when using wet or icy runways. The improved reverser consisted of two curved doors, which when not required lay faired with the engine nacelle, but when activated moved to the rear of the jet pipe to deflect the thrust. Previously internal clamshell doors were installed ahead of the tailpipe, a method inherited from the 727. Following this success all 737s delivered after March 1969 were fitted with the improved reverser, while a kit for updating earlier specimens retrospectively was made available.

Throughout 1968 work continued on devising a means to reduce further the cruising drag, which was found on test to be 5% higher than anticipated. It was responsible for a 30kt reduction in the estimated speed figures so Boeing was keen to recover this as soon as possible. Much of the deficiency had been reclaimed by the availability of the JT8D-9 engines, so at least there was no customer pressure arising from poor performance. Running parallel to these trials was a study to improve the 737's short-field capabilities. Modifications considered offered an increase of about 2,000lb (907.2kg) to the payload, or alternatively by leaving the latter unchanged, a shorter permitted take-off run was possible.

At the beginning of 1969 there were signs that Boeing was considerably stretched financially, although the order book did not reflect any cause for alarm. There was a certain degree of concern about the relatively slow sales of the 737 when compared with the rival DC-9, but nevertheless there was little to complain about because the Boeing twin-jet had already won 228 orders, of which 118 had been fulfilled. In addition the Seattle company was also busy meeting the steady demands for the 707/720 (832 ordered with 776 delivered) while 667 727s were in service with another 102 outstanding. Any drain on the company's resources was due to the enormous expense incurred in the development of the new generation 747, which was to launch the so-called Jumbo era. There was also a considerable technical effort being applied to the supersonic project, but with the ending of this programme any possible cut-backs were averted.

There was also the comforting knowledge that the ongoing programme of 737 development had been responsible for the introduction of modifications to encourage a much improved overall performance. During the studies 134 aircraft had trundled out of the hangar, so in March 1969 it was the 135th airframe which became the first to have all of the many changes incorporated on the line. Extending the engine nacelles by 45in

Above:
Transavia's 737-200 PH-TVH shows its keenness to become airborne. *AJW*

(1.14m) accompanied by better sealing of the flaps, slats and access panels along the lower leading edge of the wing, all helped to reduce the drag and increase the range. Changes were also made to the vortex generators, which together with the wing improvements and new type of thrust reverser, were offered in kit form free of

Below:
USAir became a major operator of the 737, the first of which was N310AU in 1982. *Boeing*

charge to companies possessing the earlier specimens. The combined effect of all this produced a better payload/range performance, a cruising speed in line with the original specification and an improved short-field capability.

This latter ability meant that some interested customers wanted to employ the 737 on routes that linked airports not renowned for their modern facilities. Often these sites possessed most of the ingredients for a concrete runway, cement being the most obvious absentee. Operating from gravel or unpaved strips could be a hazardous business for a jet, especially with the powerplant slung as low as that on the Boeing machine. Some form of protection against flying stones and other foreign bodies was therefore necessary, so the manufacturer developed a suitable device which was made available as a complete package for fitting by the operator.

A deflection ski attached to the nose wheel leg, was intended to discourage the sand-blasting of the lower fuselage, while similar but smaller examples were located between the main wheels for the same purpose. With this tempting target lost, the flying debris could quite rightly be expected to home in on the engine intakes to the detriment of the unit. To remove this danger a dissipator was placed at the front of each nacelle to destroy any ground level vortex and therefore the chance of ingesting unwanted material. To complete the protective exercise the various antennae below the fuselage were strengthened and the rotating anti-collision beacon was replaced by one designed to retract. All that remained before Boeing could market the kit was the seal of approval from the FAA, which was quickly forthcoming.

Towards the end of 1969 orders for the 737 of all variants had reached 257, with only 50 remaining undelivered. There was something of a lull in sales, which did little to help the company in its bid to reach the estimated production run of 600. It was therefore a good time to announce further improvements to enliven not only the performance but also the market. Using the prototype for the trials, changes to the control system included extending the leading-edge flaps and slats to produce a significant increase in lift. Take-off weights were raised by 5,000lb (2,268kg), while both stalling and approach speeds were reduced appreciably. At the same time the aircraft was employed to test a new automatic braking system. Boeing was encouraged by the comments received from those evaluating the aircraft, so steps were taken to introduce the new Advanced model of the various Series 200s from May 1971.

Once again, kits were made available for operators of the original airframes so that the

Above:
Boeing produced a deflector which when fitted to the nosewheel, prevents damage by foreign objects during operations from unpaved strips. *S. Ouzounian*

advantages of the later technology could be enjoyed. The first to appear in April 1971 contained the automatic brakes and improved anti-skid units, followed in October by the various changes to the wing's high-lift devices. Last of the series on offer concerned a nosewheel braking system. Although not a part of the retrospective changes, customers of new production aircraft were able to opt for the latest JT8D-15 turbofan developing 15,500lb (7,031kg) thrust. Using this engine the permitted maximum take-off weight for the 737 was raised to 115,500lb (52,390kg).

None of the JT8D family could claim to be particularly quiet, but excessive noise was a problem causing growing concern. In an attempt to reduce the impact upon long-suffering ears, Pratt & Whitney redesigned the engine so that one fan stage was eliminated but two compressor stages were added. At the same time the thrust rating was raised to over 16,000lb (7,257kg). Boeing was also anxious to play its part in the reduction of sound levels, so a nacelle was developed which was acoustically lined. Designed to meet the newly proposed FAA regulations, the first operator of a 737 so equipped was the Canadian carrier, Eastern Provincial, in 1973.

With the arrival of the wide-bodied types, passengers were becoming accustomed to the spaciousness of the new aircraft. While manufacturers of the single-aisle machines could not compete by physically expanding the cabin, it was certainly a feasible proposition to give this impression. By clever use of the latest materials, wall and ceiling linings were recontoured, while luggage racks became capacious bins with

non-spill doors. Concealed lighting completed the transformation, which considerably improved the actual comfort and appearance of the interior.

Thereafter minor improvements were implemented and the JT8D-17 engine came into use during the mid-1970s. By this time Boeing was engaged in studies for a possible development, but it was 1980 before any serious work started on the new Series 300 project. Eventually it was the success of this advanced model that brought an end to the -200's production run after some 18 years. During this time 1,144 had been built and delivered (including 30 Series 100s), the final example being delivered to the Chinese carrier, Xiamen Airlines, as B-2524 on 2 August 1988.

Below:
A dissipator under each nacelle prevents the engines from ingesting stones and other unwelcome objects. *S. Ouzounian*

When Lufthansa was forced to cease flying at the end of World War 2, 10 years were to pass before the German national airline was permitted to restart its operations. On 1 April 1955 the first services began, with expansion thereafter continuing at a rapid rate. Convair 340s/440s, Viscounts and Super Constellations were soon plying the growing network of routes, but the airline was already looking to the future. Boeing 707s began to take over the longer sectors in 1960 with 720s entering service a year later on the Middle East and South American runs. Neither were really ideal the intra-European routes which were still largely covered by Viscounts and Super Constellations; duties unsuited for a type intended for long-range trips.

Lufthansa chose the Boeing 727 as the replacement, the first being delivered in 1964. While it was far superior to its predecessors, even the trijet was uneconomic when employed on the short-stage German internal services. Although a marked improvement from the passenger and maintenance point of view, it had to be regarded as a stop-gap until a truly short-haul jet became available.

When Boeing began its market survey for such a machine, it therefore found an interested potential customer in Germany. With three of the US company's products already serving with the airline. Lufthansa had concluded that whenever possible a policy of standardisation would be beneficial, particularly with the high degree of commonality built into the designs by the manufacturer. During 1963 the small capacity 737 was carefully evaluated by the German carrier which was responsible for several changes in the original specification. Still seeking a candidate to launch the project, Boeing was happy to oblige and was rewarded by an order for 21 aircraft on 19 February 1965.

Assuming the timetable was maintained, deliveries were expected to begin with sufficient time left for training and service entry before the end of 1967. Unfortunately flight testing had revealed the need for various modifications to be incorporated, which in turn were responsible for some production delays. At first it was thought that an extra three months would be required, but this proved to be a pessimistic forecast.

With the necessary work completed, the first 737 (D-ABEC) was deliverd to Lufthansa at Seattle on 27 December, whereupon a concentrated programme of crew training immediately began.

While the weather in Germany could be thought seasonal, it was not particularly conducive to uninterrupted circuit flying with a brand new airliner. Therefore, instead of taking the 737 across the Atlantic to a shivering Fatherland, the airline based its new acquisition at Tucson, Az, a spot where snow and ice were unlikely to impede progress. On 4 January 1968 the conversion training started for the first of some 90 pilots due to take the course. Thereafter the aircraft was kept busy, because the schedule called for in excess of 11hr/day in the air to be regularly punctuated by 40 touch-and-gos and 10 full-stop landings.

By the time that the first batch of aircrews were fully conversant with the type, Boeing had delivered a second specimen to Lufthansa. Marketed as 'City Jet' by the carrier to complement the 727 'Europa Jets', its arrival enabled the airline to introduce the 737 into service from the operations base at Frankfurt on 10 February. The first task was to take over the domestic sectors from the trijets, so it was not long before nine West German airports (Bremen, Cologne, Dusseldorf, Frankfurt, Hamburg, Hanover, Munich, Nurnburg and Stuttgart) were added to its workload. This rapid expansion was possible because Boeing was now in the position to promise deliveries at frequent intervals, to take the number on strength by August to 15. Once this level had been reached, Lufthansa was able to turn its attention to routes linking the German cities with neighbouring countries.

Passenger reaction to the 737 was extremely favourable, although because of the much reduced time taken to complete some of the short internal flights, meals were understandably no longer offered. As compensation the cabin was laid out with only 84 seats at 34in pitch compared with the possible 96. With the aid of the fore and aft airstairs, rapid turnrounds were being achieved; a necessity if the machines were to cover an average of seven sectors each day.

Surprisingly, the first Series 200 was delivered only two days after the initial Lufthansa machine, N9002U pioneering the United Airlines' fleet. Crew training accounted for much of the next four months so it was not until 29 April 1968 that the airline introduced the type to its scheduled services, by which time six were on strength.

Another carrier amongst the early customers was Britannia Airways. In 1965 it was already considering which jet type would suit its special requirements, bearing in mind its intensive IT

work to the Mediterranean. BAC was confident that its One-Eleven would be chosen, thereby following the example of British Eagle and Court, both of which were involved in the same type of business. But it was not to be. Britannia preferred the economics offered by the Boeing jet which could not be equalled by the One-Eleven. The latter's fuselage dimensions really only supported a five-abreast cabin, although there was an offer to change this to six in a desperate attempt to win the order. As a precedent Channel Airways was cited, a carrier which also managed to squeeze seven-abreast seating into a Trident before the age of twin-aisles. By the end of a journey the occupants had become good friends!

At Seattle the prospect of an order from the UK airline provided unusual interest because it was the first time that the company had been involved in the affairs of an IT charter carrier. A longer range was essential and the interior had to be adapted for a high-density layout, but at the same time space had to be found for the carrying of duty-free goods etc. Against considerable pressure from the British government and BAC, Britannia decided to order three 737s (with one option) for delivery in the spring of 1968. Nowadays manufacturers are willing to cover the certification costs involved in gaining this seal of approval for their products, but in the 1960s the cost had to be borne by the airline. In addition, a 14% charge was imposed by the UK government under the Import Duty Act of 1958, although this could have been waived in the absence of a suitable alternative. Naturally Britannia argued that this was so, whereas the Civil Servants claimed that the One-Eleven would be satisfactory.

With the delivery date drawing near, preparations were well in hand for the 737's participation in the summer programme when news of the production delays reached Luton. Unlike scheduled operators, Britannia's capacity was sold in advance to the travel trade so the company was in a difficult position. To cover the shortage it was necessary to lease the Britannia 102 G-ANBN from Laker for the season, fortunately at Boeing's expense. At last the long-awaited moment arrived when the 737-200 G-AVRL touched down at its future home base on 8 July 1968 after its trip from Seattle.

Stops were made at Montreal and Goose Bay, Labrador, before the direct Atlantic crossing to Luton carrying some Boeing instructors in addition to Britannia personnel. Five flight-deck crews were partially trained at Seattle, but the conversion work was completed in Britain with the pilots loaned by the manufacturer. With a second machine due in August, another batch of six crews quickly began their training at the Bedfordshire headquarters in readiness for the arrival. In the meantime Romeo Lima flew the company's inaugural sortie on 22 July to Dubrovnik, Jugoslavia, albeit an outing for 115 invited guests. For its initial revenue-earning excursion the aircraft visited Alicante a few days later.

The airline had specified an all-tourist, 117-seat configuration for its latest equipment, particularly convenient because its seven Britannias also had this capacity. Nonetheless there were already plans to increase the total carried in the 737s after 1969 to 124, which would reduce the pitch to 31in. Manufactured in the UK, the new seats and the proposed layout were also approved by the FAA, an important step because Britannia hoped to

Above:
Britannia began operating the 737 in 1968, G-AVRM being the second received. *G. W. Pennick*

lease the aircraft in the US during the slack winter periods.

There is little doubt that the UK airline's experience with the 737, coupled with the aircraft's performance in this highly specialised field, set such an example that Boeing began to reap the benefit in the form of orders. Although a member of the Thomson Group, Britannia did not rely entirely on the tour operator for its business. Winter holidays were still in their infancy, so in order to keep the fleet active some diversification was necessary. Military contracts provided useful employment for the 737s because some 17 flights each week took the aircraft to and from Germany with members of the forces and their families. In the early 1970s Britannia also used the aircraft for long-haul charters, which found them as far afield as Singapore and Hong Kong.

By the end of 1971 the airline had replaced all its turboprop Britannias with 737s. Eight of the type were now in service to cope with the rapidly growing number of people abandoning the rain and wind-swept British seaside resorts for the promise of the sun-scorched Mediterranean area. More 737s were added for the 1974 summer

Below:
One of six Series 200s delivered in 1980, G-BGYL was named *Jean Batten* before entering service.
G. W. Pennick

season to take the total to 14, this number then remaining constant until 1977 as a result of one of the government's regular economic crises causing a temporary pause in the growth. During the winter months, short-term leases for some of the 737s provided work and welcome income, but the rapid expansion of the industry by the late 1970s soon brought the need for additional capacity. In the 1982 peak period no fewer than 29 737s were operated by Britannia plus five that were leased from Transavia. Quebecair and Eagle Air. In March of the following year Boeing delivered what was to be the last new 737 (G-BKHF) to be acquired by the UK airline, although the arrival was countered by the disposal of an older pair.

Each year the number of passengers carried had beaten previous records, a trend which was continuing. The 737s had long been configured with 130 seats, but the time was approaching when a larger machine was needed to complement the faithful Boeing. Several alternatives were considered, but undoubtedly the close relationship built up through the years between the US manufacturer and Britannia contributed to the choice of the 767 over the Airbus equivalent. In February 1984 the first of the new generation jets arrived at Luton and immediately its 273-seat layout eased any capacity shortage.

With four in use to handle the 1985 summer traffic, it was possible to begin the reduction of the 737 fleet either by selling or by means of long leases. Nevertheless there were still 27 in service although three more had left the company by 1987, ironically making it necessary to lease in several examples as a temporary measure in order to cope with the peak period.

By this time the 737-300 series had been introduced by Boeing, but Britannia took no steps to replace its fleet with the later model. However, subsequent events were to change this decision because in 1988 the news was released that the Thomson Group had bought Horizon. This meant that Orion Airways, together with its fleet of 737-300s, would be absorbed into Britannia. Integration took some time to complete, but 1989 saw the latter operating the repainted, larger and quieter version alongside the original aircraft after all.

Below:
Two 737-200C convertibles joined Britannia in 1970. One was G-AXNA, seen many years later in the scheme of the day. During 1989 the company's engineering centre began one of the most comprehensive airframe overhauls to be undertaken by an airline. It took nine months to complete and when X-ray Alpha emerged in April 1990 it carred the legend 'The first Boeing to be made in England' in recognition of the achievement by the UK company. *AJW*

Back in the 1960s it was obvious that if the planned very high utilisation was to be possible, an efficient maintenance facility was required. This became even more essential as the fleet steadily increased in size, so purpose-built accommodation for the engineering division was erected alongside Luton's apron. Space for four 737s was provided — five with the hangar door partially open — to cater for the constant flow of aircraft as they became due for checks.

Major overhauls obviously keep the machine grounded for the longest period and are started by positioning the 737 into the tail docking rig. Independent contractors remove all the paint-work overnight so that by the next morning the airframe is down to bare metal. Without delay all major components are removed from the jacked-up machine for individual overhaul in the appropriate specialist workshop on the site. Meanwhile the remaining structure is subjected to a thorough X-ray investigation to ensure that there are no signs of cracking in the skin or frames. Other non-destructive tests using ultra-sonic and eddy current techniques enable any corrosion areas to be detected, the results eventually being used to formulate the nature of the remedial work required on the overhaul.

While the repairs are underway, the opportunity is also taken to incorporate any modifications advised in the regular Boeing service bulletins before reassembly begins. Gradually the inspected and overhauled items are returned to meet the pre-arranged timetable until the 737 is restored and ready for repainting. Once it has been sprayed, the aircraft is removed from its dock in readiness for engine runs, weighed and air tested for re-certification.

Naturally the majority of the engineering facility's time is devoted to the welfare of Britannia's own aircraft, but nonetheless a considerable amount of third-party work is also carried out for other carriers. Such business has been won by establishing an excellent reputation over many years, as reflected by the airline's impressive record of reliability.

Britannia remained the only UK 737 operator for some 11 years, until in 1979 the newly formed Air Europe took delivery of its first examples, to be quickly followed by Orion and British Airways. Thereafter the type was adopted by other carriers as they attempted to win a share of the air transport boom. If they failed it was rarely the 737's fault.

Below:
Air Europe became a 737 operator in 1979 and quickly entered into an aircraft exchange agreement with Air Florida. This is well depicted by N54AF and G-BMSM seen together in their own livery but with titles transposed. *Air Europe*

Throughout the 1970s Boeing's sales team managed to attract a steady flow of orders for the 737-200, until by the end of the decade the aircraft was the company's fastest-selling type. In fact its success was indeed fortunate, because in the midst of a deep recession there was little other good news. During 1979 the figures received a welcome boost when Lufthansa decided to replace its entire fleet of Series 100s with 32 of the latest Advanced 200 variant. Meanwhile, although the latter's popularity showed no signs of waning, Boeing was already preparing for the future by exploring feasible developments for the basic airframe.

When some of the first details of the proposed Series 300 were released in 1980, it was apparent that the manufacturer had managed to provide extra capacity in a modestly stretched fuselage, but the main benefits were to be derived from utilising modern, quieter but larger engines without the need for expensive and lengthy redesign of the wing. At this stage no definite decision had been taken, but if a go-ahead was to be given, the timing of its production and flight trials would have to be adjusted to match the progress of the brand new powerplant.

Whether the 300 remained a paper exercise depended very much upon sufficient orders being received to justify a launch. By the spring of 1981 the regional carrier, USAir, was expected to be amongst the first to sign for the extended 737, but Boeing would still need more support before firmly committing itself to the project. In the event Southwest Airlines was also prepared to become a lead customer, whereupon both companies ordered 10 examples, as well as taking options on another 20. It was an unusually small number to precipitate a go-ahead decision, but the willingness of the manufacturer to accept this situation could be explained by the relatively low development cost anticipated ($250 million) and the size of the envisaged future market.

Any scheme for updating the 737 to reduce noise and fuel usage was difficult to achieve without losing some of the attractive features of the aircraft. In order to compensate for the substitution of heavier engines with more generous proportions, a wing extension using a new centre-section would normally be the answer. This could not be done with wing-mounted powerplants without a complete redesign, something that Boeing wished to avoid. Similarly for the same reason it was only practical to add a very small extension to the wing tips. As if this was not enough, the extra capacity introduced to help defray the increased cost of the aircraft added to the weight penalties. At an early stage it was calculated that there would inevitably be a significant rise in landing speeds until the point could be reached where they were unacceptable.

Back in the 1960s Boeing had devised a neat method for hanging the two slim JT8Ds snugly under the 737's wings. An identical arrangement could not be used for the new generation engines, which by necessity had to be fatter to be quieter. Presented with all these problems, there

appeared no easy way to overcome them without
forfeiting some of the advantages. It was
concluded that the powerplant held the key, so
Boeing approached CFM International in the hope
that a joint effort would produce a solution.

Previously the Seattle company had worked
with the engine manufacturer when attempts
were being made to interest carriers in a
re-engined 707. One CFM56-powered civil example was completed for trials and demonstration
work, but no orders were forthcoming so the
project was dropped. However, the combination
proved popular for military versions of the
four-engined jet, which ensured a life extension
for the veterans. This association with the CFM56
and its creator proved very helpful, so by early
1980 the general design for a closely-cowled wing
mounted engine was well advanced.

Development of the CFM56 began in the early
1970s, although the first did not run until June
1974. A McDonnell Douglas YC-15 became the
test bed for the turbofan's flight trials, carrying
the engine in its port outer pod from February
1977. A Caravelle was similarly employed in
France, but in this case the CFM56 occupied the
starboard nacelle. In 1978 the long-awaited
commercial orders were received when airlines
began to retrofit their DC-8s. At this time the
engine was known as the CFM56-2 and was rated
at 24,000lb thrust, but plans were already in hand
to offer a smaller version with correspondingly
reduced power to be designated 56-3. Chosen to
power the 737-300, work proceeded on the
scaled-down engine with the first bench runs
being scheduled for the spring of 1982. Subject to
satisfactory results, Edwards AFB was earmarked
as the scene of the three-month flight trials due to
begin a year or so later using a 707 converted for
the purpose.

Even on the earlier 737s the ground clearance
beneath the JT8D's nacelle was small but

Above:
The eventual nacelle and intake design for the CFM56 is apparent in this shot of Air Europe's 737-300 G-BNPA climbing away. *G. W. Pennick*

sufficient. One possible solution to the problem of hanging the larger unit under the wing was to extend the length of the main undercarriage legs, but this would have meant another redesign, bringing greater cost and weight. Normally much of the ancillary equipment was located on the top or bottom of the engine, but in order to reduce the height of the 56-3, CFM relocated these accessories on the two sides. When wrapped in its nacelle an oval shape was produced which included a flattened underside for good measure.

Despite this ingenuity it was still too big to be fitted in the same manner as the JT8D, but this was overcome by attaching the nacelle to a pylon so that the bulk was close to, but actually ahead of the wing's leading edge. To avoid overheating the undersurface and trailing edge flaps, the entire assembly was slightly raised at the front so that the exhaust was deflected downwards. Not only satisfying the ground clearance requirements, the new method of installation provided more space for fuel in the wing. Hitherto the area directly

Below:
CFM56 engine mounting, 737-300/400/500.

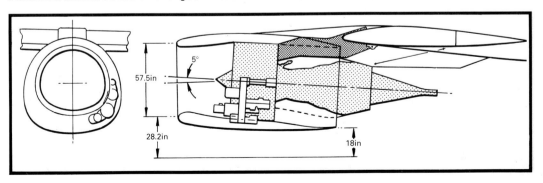

above the engines could not house a tank because of the close fitting nacelles.

Boeing had always resolved to keep any wing design changes to a minimum, so generally the structure remained similar to that of the earlier series. In addition to strengthening the section carrying the pylons, due to the different engine mounting system, attention had to be given to the elimination of possible flutter between the wing and powerplant. With the weight suspended on the pylon there was a tendency for a twisting action to exert itself, although this was normally corrected by stiffening the appropriate section of the structure during manufacture. Under the circumstances this would be costly and time-consuming, so a proven alternative was substituted which consisted of a weighted probe at each wingtip. These were designed to increase the natural frequency between the engines and the mainplane, therefore removing the risk of flutter. Ironically, after carefully devising the method, Boeing found that there was no need to use the probes after all, so they were removed before the first flight.

To counter the effects of the additional weight on approach speeds, the manufacturer introduced a new leading-edge slat. Extending from the pylon to the wingtip, it was more than twice the size of that fitted to the -200 and increased the chord by an average of 4% over the whole wing.

The modified aerofoil section of the device not only enabled the approach speed to be reduced to a figure only 5kt higher than that of the -200, but also added another 4,000ft of cruising altitude, a most satisfactory bonus.

Changes to the fuselage were kept to a minimum, but it was lengthened by 104in (2.64m) with the aid of a 44in (1.12m) plug just forward of the wing, plus a second measuring 60in (1.52m) adjacent to the trailing edge. Within the cabin the number of emergency exits provided determined that the maximum capacity allowed under the FAA regulations was 149 seats. In reality the precise total varied with the configuration. While a 30in-pitch, six-abreast arrangement was normal for all-tourist layouts, when a first class cabin was provided its eight seats were located in pairs either side of the aisle. The number and whereabouts of toilets and galleys again depended upon the operator's own wishes, but could be permutated at the front and rear of the passenger accommodation.

Crushed core honeycomb material was employed for many of the interior components, using a method originally developed for the 757. It enabled larger, modern styled, overhead baggage bins to be installed, while lighting was

Below:
Boeing 737-300.

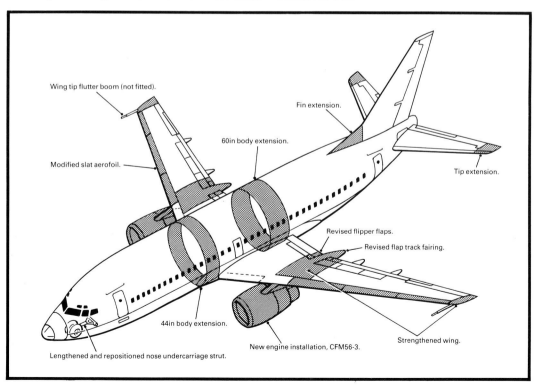

Wing tip flutter boom (not fitted).

Fin extension.

60in body extension.

Modified slat aerofoil.

Tip extension.

Revised flipper flaps.

Revised flap track fairing.

44in body extension.

Strengthened wing.

New engine installation, CFM56-3.

Lengthened and repositioned nose undercarriage strut.

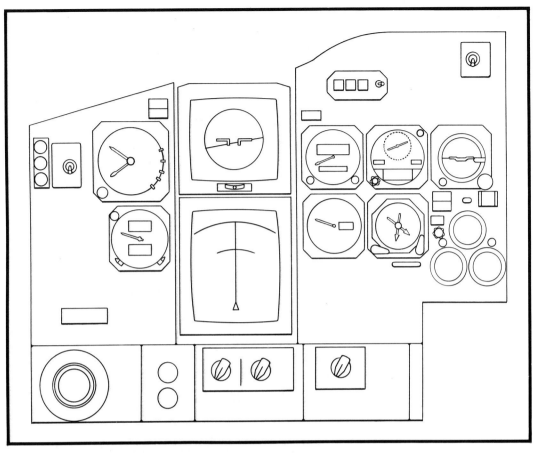

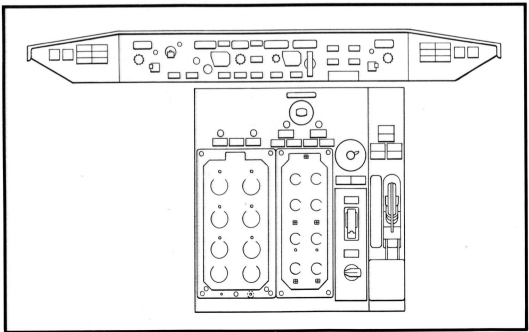

also greatly improved. These advanced techniques were also incorporated into all new 737-200s from the beginning of 1984 to maintain the manufacturer's practice to update earlier products whenever practical.

Boeing endeavoured to retain a marked similarity between the cockpits of the two models, thereby allowing a common type rating for pilots. Nevertheless, a certain number of new features were introduced, including flight management and digital flight control systems, but the company resisted the temptation to instal cathode-ray tube displays instead of the traditional electro-mechanical instruments. Apparently there had been little demand shown for the change.

At the rear of the fuselage the dorsal fin was slightly enlarged to meet the effects of the greater asymmetric thrust, while both the tailplane and elevators were also increased in size. At the other end the twin-nosewheel assembly was repositioned slightly to play its part in the ground clearance exercise, which, when completed, produced a distance of 28in between the inlet and the concrete, only 2in less than that enjoyed by the -200.

Despite the -300's obvious technical advances, Boeing did not regard it as a replacement for its older brethren. Indeed, in April 1982 the company was able to announce the sale of the 1,000th 737, this milestone being reached following an order for seven -200s from Air Portugal. While the demand continued there was certainly no point in

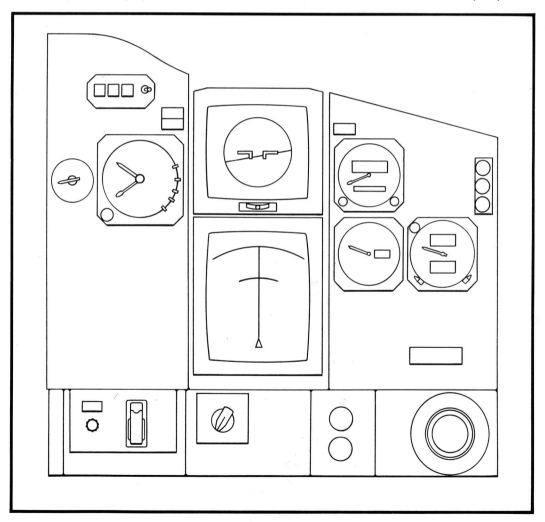

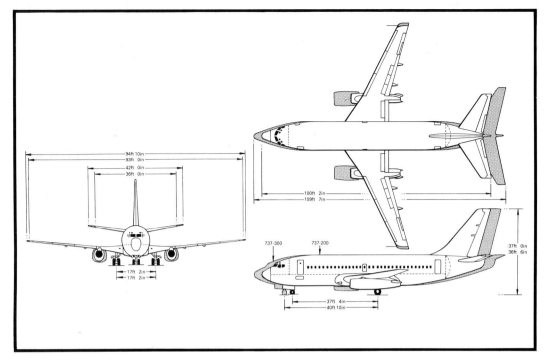

Above:
Size comparison 737-200/300.

ending the production run, especially since the -300 had broken no records for sales. In fact they had remained rather stagnant with the launch customers remaining the only names in the order book one year later.

This somewhat dismal picture did not unduly perturb Boeing because it recognised that many users of the type were small carriers unaccustomed to placing large orders years in advance. The company's patience was rewarded in mid-1982 when the UK charter airline Orion Airways placed five firm orders plus a number of options. Four aircraft were specified for delivery in 1985 with the fifth to follow during the next year — later deferred until 1988. Although the machines were to be used on IT work, Orion declined the maximum 149 seats in favour of 144 plus a third toilet. It was something of a distinction for the airline to become the first outside the US to order the type.

Later in the year the company took an unusual step by ordering a 737-300 simulator from Rediffusion. Normally, operators of Orion's size do not invest in such a machine, preferring instead to pay for training at other sites. However, it was specified that a rapid reconfiguration to suit -200 aircraft would be possible, a useful feature bearing in mind that the carrier also operated this variant. Once installed and on line in 1985, the

simulator was more than adequate for Orion's needs, so sessions were sold to other operators until the unit was almost continuously in use. This success later prompted the purchase of a second simulator, but on this occasion the Singer Link-Miles product equipped with electronic instrumentation was chosen.

February 1983 found the -300 taking shape in Boeing's workshops. At Wichita, work was well advanced on wing, body and thrust reverser parts, while in California the Rohr Corporation had started on the engine inlet and side cowlings. A full-size metal mock-up to precise measurements had been built at Renton so that the electrical wiring and hydraulic tubing runs could be checked before becoming a pattern for production machines.

No unforeseen difficulties were encountered during the assembly of the prototype, so as predicted several years earlier, all was ready to present the 737-300 to the world on 17 January 1984. Such opportunities are never overlooked in the US where roll-out ceremonies are professionally organised. This was no exception. When the huge curtains were drawn back, the latest highly-polished Boeing creation was seen under a galaxy of coloured lights as it slowly rotated on its platform before an audience of 10,000. It was almost too much for the over-sensitive.

All that was left to complete was the ground running of the CFM56s, a task expected to be

Above:
An early flight for the prototype 737-300 as the fuselage is lifted into position to join the waiting wings. *Boeing*

Left:
Safely lined up, the 737-300 is ready for the next stage. In the background are two Series 200s for USAir. *Boeing*

completed so that the 1,001st 737 could make its maiden flight on 2 March. The allocated period proved to be too generous because on the morning of 24 February, the -300 took to the air from Renton with Jim McRoberts in command and Tom Edmonds as co-pilot. This initial sortie lasted 2hr 56min, during which the machine reached a maximum altitude of 29,000ft. As customary on these occasions, the pilots proceeded to check the handling characteristics, flight controls, undercarriage operation and basic systems before landing N73700 at Boeing Field, the base for the forthcoming trials. It was not the first use of this registration because the original prototype Series 100 also carried the mark back in the late 1960s. Only a week or so elapsed before the second -300 left the ground for the first time, to spend 2hr 58min aloft on 2 March. Registered N351AU, this specimen was painted in the colours of USAir, its future owner at the conclusion of its test activities. It took only a

month for the pair to accrue 80hr of flying to the complete satisfaction of the manufacturer. One of the early investigations concerned the engine/wing flutter characteristics, but the precautionary addition of a 110lb weight in each wing proved unnecessary and was quickly removed. This supported the original decision to discard the wingtip probes intended for the same purpose.

Included in the total was some engine certification work carried out by N73700 during a visit to Grant County Airport at Moses Lake, followed by high altitude trials at Colorado Springs with FAA personnel in attendance at both locations. Upon its return to its home base, the prototype joined its partner for low-speed handling tests which embraced such items as drag, stalls, trimming and manoeuvring.

Now that the -300 had flown and was already confirming the maker's claims, sales began to pick up. Already the operator of 63 Series 200s, Piedmont decided to add 15 of the larger version to its inventory. Of these, 10 were specified in 138-seat configuration with the remaining five intended for mixed-class operations with accommodation for 128 passengers. Boeing also won a 10-strong order from the International Lease Finance Corporation, the first time that the manufacturer had received such a boost from an organisation that was neither an airline nor government agency.

By November 1984 the total number of firm orders held for the -300 had reached 155 shared between 13 different customers. In the same

Above:
Flight trials soon began with the 737-300 registered N73700. *Boeing*

month US certification was obtained at the conclusion of nine months test flying; the three aircraft involved logging 1,294hr in the process. After the results of the work had been analysed, it was clear that the type's performance exceeded expectations and was even more fuel efficient than predicted. Its FAA approval also meant that the -300 met the latest noise limits for take-off, sideline and approach sounds.

There was now nothing to prevent deliveries beginning. Consequently both USAir and South-west Airlines received their first machines before the end of the month, the latter operating the inaugural revenue service by a 737-300 when N300SW took over a scheduled run from Houston on 7 December.

Since the third customer was Orion, it was immediately necessary to secure a type certificate from the CAA if the carrier was to be able to introduce its new possessions at an early date. Fortunately there were no difficulties encoun-tered, so the way was clear for the airline to take delivery of its first example in early February 1985, the remainder of the four-strong fleet joining it at East Midlands by the end of March. Unlike similar aircraft in the US, the British contingent was employed on IT work. Operating

alongside the depleted ranks of Series 200s in the airline's employ, the -300s helped to carry 1,065,000 passengers during 1985. From the company's point of view the aircraft was proving a good investment, especially since it was using 24% less fuel than the older -200s, a 3% improvement on Boeing's estimates. Dispatch reliability during the first six months averaged 99% with load factors of 90% and a utilisation of 9hr/day. The management also had every hope that the CFM56's quietness would help to reduce the night movement restrictions currently enforced.

As 1985 progressed, new developments were made available to the 737 customers. In response to a request made initially by Trans Australian, Boeing offered the option of electronic flight instruments, which were duly certificated by the FAA on 24 July 1986. Higher maximum take-off weights were also possible following the introduction of the more powerful CFM56-3B2 engines of 22,000lb thrust.

Naturally it is reasonable to assume that most airliners are destined to carry fare-paying passengers from point-to-point. While this is generally the case, there are exceptions when the machine is corporately or even privately owned. Boeing recognised this somewhat thin market for its wares especially in view of the growing trend to convert retired 727s for executive travel. For this reason both the 737-200 and -300 were made available as the Corporate 77-32 and -33 respectively. However, in due course the designations were revised to become 737-200 Corporate and 737-300 Corporate in a similar manner to the 747, 757 and 767 executive variants.

First sale of the -300 model was made at the 1986 National Business Aircraft Association convention held at Anaheim, Ca. With a capacity for about 20 passengers within its capacious fuselage, a degree of comfort could be expected. This was indeed so, because included in the list of facilities on board was a conference room, bedroom, dining room with appropriate catering arrangements and a bathroom.

Towards the end of the decade, the 737-300 became increasingly popular with the airlines, a fact confirmed by the total on order having risen to 853 by September 1989, of which 560 had been delivered. Nevertheless, long before the variant first flew in February 1984, Boeing had already begun to concentrate its thoughts on the future, and a 150-seater in particular.

Left:
Dan-Air's first 737-300 G-SCUH pauses to illustrate the limited gap between the nacelle and the ground.
AJW

At the beginning of the 1980s there were already murmurings about the need for a new-technology airliner in the 130-160 seat range. In Boeing's opinion this market was some years distant and in the interim period would be served by the recently announced 737-300, although even this development was not due to enter service until 1984. When the time came to offer a slightly larger machine, the company already knew that it had two possible options, both involving some surgery to an existing model. Despite previous denials when the subject was aired, one of Boeing's schemes was to reduce the size of the narrow-bodied 757 to suit the new specification. Alternatively the company considered that it was practical to give the 737 yet another stretch without undue expense.

By 1982 there was another factor to further complicate the issue when Boeing released the news that it intended to launch a new 150-seat airliner as the 7-7. The announcement went on to confirm that the development of the 737 would continue in the meantime because it could be made available much sooner than the proposed newcomer. None of this was taken very seriously by the industry because it was generally thought that it would not be possible to enlarge the 737-300 without a complete redesign of the wing, a very costly exercise for something merely intended as a stop-gap. Needless to say, such thoughts did not deter Boeing from going ahead with some preliminary outline work for its latest venture.

In parallel with the 737 derivative, by 1984 studies were also actively underway into two possible products for the future 150-seat market. The latest project to emerge was slightly smaller than the 7-7 and was to be powered by twin rear-mounted propfans. Engines of this type were still some years away from commercial service, so Boeing was not expecting to offer the machine until 1992 at the earliest. Already some customers were somewhat sceptical about this target, bearing in mind the considerable amount of advanced technology proposed for the design. Lufthansa was one such operator that could not afford to assume that the development processes would be completed within the timescale, but in any case it would be too late for the carrier's own planned replacement programme. Airbus Industrie therefore won an order for 15 A320s from the German airline because at least this aircraft was a reality and would be available from 1988.

Continued success for the European manufacturer meant that Boeing's contender had to be a step ahead in terms of modern techniques, so the company decided to drop the 7-7. Had it survived, the airliner would have been very similar in concept to the A320 and therefore offered few advantages. It left the way clear for the company to concentrate on the unducted fan (UDF) project which was by 1985 no longer merely a dream. Indeed Boeing was convinced that when the order book for the 7J7 – as it was now designated – was opened, it would quickly outsell the A320. This step was expected in late 1986 or early in the new year, with a foreign airline becoming one of the launch customers.

It was all rather confusing because at the time the 737-300 was selling extremely well and there was still talk about the Series 400. To avoid losing too many orders to Airbus during the lengthy wait for the 7J7, Boeing decided to proceed with the latest 737 variant, which would help the company to retain its grip on the 150-seat market, but at the same time reduce the pressure on the development of the UDF machine.

Some six years had passed since the prospect of another 737 stretch had first been contemplated, but throughout the period the design team had not been idle. Consequently when sales surveys indicated that it would be sensible to go ahead with the project, all was ready for the preparation of the detailed drawings – subject, of course, to the procurement of a launch customer. In June 1986 the necessary supporter was found when Piedmont placed an order for 25 aircraft with 30 options; a batch certainly sufficient for Boeing to confidently continue with all speed.

As much of the Series 300's technology as possible was used for the latest family member, the main difference concerning the fuselage which was extended by a further 10ft (3.05m). To achieve this a 6ft (1.83m) plug was inserted forward of the wing, with another of 4ft (1.22m) to the rear; when the Series 300 was announced there was a consensus of opinion which thought a redesign of the wing would be essential. To the surprise of the observers this was proved not to be the case, but this time was different. With such an increase in size there was no way to avoid the issue – or so it seemed.

Once again Boeing confounded the experts by retaining the original wing in a strengthened form to cope with the higher maximum landing weight of 121,000lb (55,000kg), compared with 114,000lb

Above:
This view of the Renton line shows a mix of 737-300s and -400s including the first two (G-BNKA/B) of the latter for Air Europe in the foreground. *Boeing*

(51,820kg) for the Series 300. The chord was increased by 4% to gain some 18kt cruising speed, while better braking was achieved by means of an extra spoiler each side. Apart from supporting the slightly extended span tailplane, the underside of the rear fuselage also sprouted a bumper to guard against damage from scrapes in the event of over enthusiastic rotations. This item was deemed desirable following experience with the even longer 757, which collected 25 such ground contacts in its first 3½ years of service.

Seating capacity was naturally increased significantly to take the standard layout to about 156, although in an all-tourist configuration the maximum could be raised to around 170. Power for the aircraft was provided by two CFM56-3B2 engines developing 22,000lb thrust, similar to those available as an option for the -300. Alternatively the 23,500lb thrust CFM56-3C could be specified, as could the brand new IAE V2500.

From the outset a higher gross weight of 150,000lb (68,040kg) was on offer, which improved the range performance appreciably. Whereas the standard Series 400 could carry 146 passengers to the Eastern Mediterranean resorts

Above:
An impression of spaciousness is given by the -400's cabin, despite the 170 seats carried. *AJW*

with ease, the heavier example could include Gander in its coverage. Interestingly the newcomer's payload/range figures were comparable with the early 707s for the price of two engines instead of four. These transatlantic sorties were made possible by obtaining the authority's approval for extended-range twin engine operations (Erops) over water. Certainly the CFM56 in its various forms had already proved itself extremely reliable, with shutdowns fewer than 0.01/1,000hr. A crumb of comfort perhaps for those preferring to see four nacelles under the wing.

The pods on the -400 were mounted in a similar manner to those of its predecessor. When the -300 was first introduced it was not absolutely certain that the low-slung units would not become a receptacle for foreign objects, despite the carefully designed shape and position. Once in service this fear was proved to be unfounded, since the flattened lower edge of the intake removed the need for any special vortex device such as that provided on the JT8Ds.

Early customers for the Series 300 were quite content for the flight-deck to contain orthodox instrumentation so Boeing did not force a change to the more modern but expensive CRT displays. Gradually the orders received began to specify the advanced cockpits, a development brought about mainly by the influence of Ansett and Lufthansa. It therefore followed that the -400 was equipped with CRTs and other digital devices from the beginning, to produce a layout very similar to that of the 757/767 and of course its smaller brethren in the 737 family. Flat-panel engine instruments supplied by Smiths Industries replaced 21 electro-mechanical counterparts, leading to easier maintenance and monitoring of performance. Once the system had been flight tested, it was cleared for use in the Series 300, for which retrofits were possible.

Roll-out of the -400 had been promised for January 1988 at the time of its launch some 18 months earlier, so with Boeing's past record in mind it was not surprising that the aircraft was ready for its public debut on schedule. Always keen on showmanship, this time the company made aviation history on 26 January by unveiling two new-model passenger airliners on the same day. In a mid-morning ceremony the 737-400 appeared before a vast audience of invited guests and employees. There were ample demonstrations of electronic wizardry as the laser lights and synthesized music assailed the senses of the assembled multitude, but this was only stage one.

At a given signal numerous buses appeared to convey the visitors from the Renton lakeside facility to Everett, the 30-mile-distant birthplace of the 747-400. The journey brought only a temporary respite from the cacophony of noise, because upon arrival once more lights and sound blasted forth to herald the appearance of the mighty machine before an even larger throng. It was indeed a remarkable feat of organisation but it will be a long time before circumstances provide the opportunity for a similar double premiere.

As preparations were made for the latest 737 model's maiden flight, Boeing was able to announce that it had already received 88 orders from nine customers, who between them also held options on a further 35 machines. Perhaps by contrived coincidence, launch airline Piedmont took delivery of its 96th 737 on the day of the -400 roll-out. Had it been two weeks or so later the type's 20th year of commercial service could also have been celebrated; it all starting with Lufthansa on 10 February 1968 and the Series 130 D-ABED. By the time of the anniversary this particular machine had since flown over 30,000hr and made some 37,000 landings during its career, which now continued in New Zealand.

Meanwhile, the infant Series 400 began its flight trials on 19 February when the aircraft became airborne for the first time at 10.05, just under four years after a similar excursion was made by the -300. As on that occasion, the pilot in command was Jim McRoberts, so he was in a good position to observe any significant handling differences. After a 1hr 45min routine trip around the area to reach 31,000ft at a fairly modest speed of 280mph, the crew were able to confirm that handling characteristics were virtually unchanged. This also applied to the registration carried, because the company's favourite 737 identity (N73700) was in use for the third time having long been shed by the previous holder, the prototype -300.

As the 400hr flight programme began in earnest to meet the certification target date in September, Boeing disclosed the fact that orders for the 737 had now passed the 2,000 mark, the most ever received for a commercial jet airliner. This notable landmark was reached following the sale of four Series 300s to the Dutch carrier Transavia, plus a massive batch of 50 for USAir; the first 20 to be Series 300s with deliveries commencing in April 1989. Although some of the remainder were also expected to be this version, the airline deferred a decision on precise numbers until both the -400 and -500 variants were available.

Across the Atlantic the Airbus A320 had just gained its type certificate, not only on time, but also to meet the new stringent European joint system. As a result the 150-seat airliner was approved simultaneously by the authorities in France, Britain, Germany and the Netherlands. With its 7J7 UDF project now postponed into the late 1990s, Boeing was no doubt relieved that it had taken the decision to develop the 737 still further. At least the Series 400 would only be six months behind its main competitor.

Above:
Air UK Leisure was the first European carrier to take delivery of the Series 400 when G-UKLA arrived in October 1988. *Boeing*

Two aircraft were employed in the trials during the summer of 1988, when 535hr were spent in the air. Their efforts were rewarded in September when the type was duly certificated by the FAA to carry up to 188 passengers. Fortunately for future travellers, Boeing expected the standard layout to contain 146 seats in a mixed-class cabin when used for scheduled services, rising to 170 for charter work. Receipt of the approval meant that deliveries to the lead customer could begin within days, so Piedmont accordingly received its first (N406US) on 15 September. Three more of the breed were taken on strength before the end of the month to allow the company – which was now a subsidiary of USAir – to introduce its latest equipment to the network.

In Europe the distinction for becoming the first operator of the 737-400 fell to Air UK Leisure, a new carrier launched in April 1988. Owned by the GPA Group, the third production aircraft was one of the three leased by Leisure from the Ireland-based company. Registered G-UKLA, the machine was formally handed over to the British airline at Seattle on 14 October, three days before

its 9½hr ferry flight to East Midlands. Here Orion was due to instal a forward galley to increase the number carried to three, plus the completion of several other refinements required by the operator. At the same time the outstanding modifications to meet the CAA's special regulations were also implemented, the remainder having been included by the manufacturer, albeit at a greater cost. In total $350,000 was spent in putting the Series 400 on to the UK register, all of which was borne by the airline.

After a week or so Lima Alpha was ready for its CAA test flight; a 3hr sortie which was concluded uneventfully on 25 October. One last hurdle remained. In order to prove that it was capable of operating the type, the company was obliged to fly a simulated service to the satisfaction of the authority. Schiphol was chosen as the target for the purposes of this exercise, so later in the day the -400 left its Stansted base for a swift return journey to the Dutch airport. With this completed without hitch, the way was clear for some intensive crew training throughout the following day, before the aircraft's inaugural commercial Faro-bound departure at 10.20 on 27 October.

Thereafter the -400 was kept busy on ITs to the Canaries and various charters including a regular series to Moscow and Leningrad. Strangely enough, at this stage Boeing seemed somewhat

41

unsure of the variant's range with maximum payload plus the necessary reserves. However, Leisure expected it to comfortably reach destinations such as Tel Aviv with 170 passengers on board, a performance which would be particularly useful when operating from the more northerly Manchester outstation.

Within the cabin the seats were arranged in a three-abreast formation apart from those adjacent to the four emergency exits. In this case those nearest to the wall were removed for ease of access. Outside, the upper surface of the wing close to the fuselage was painted white with a number of black arrows indicating the path for escaping passengers in the event of a mass evacuation.

In the spring of 1989 Air UK Leisure received its second Series 400 in time for the summer season, followed in July by the third leased example. While they were all gainfully employed on ITs and scheduled services, there were signs that the travel industry was about to suffer a severe recession. In the autumn an 18-month lease in Malaysia was negotiated for G-UKLA, while arrangements were made for the latest member of the fleet (G-UKLE) to spend the 1989/90 winter in Canada with Vacationair. Unfortunately the latter ceased operations, but at least the 737 escaped the inconvenience of being impounded. Leisure only had sufficient work contracted to keep one aircraft active until the 1990 summer programme began, a point when the first of its own machines was also due for delivery. It was a difficult time for all airlines with no immediate prospects of improvement. Nevertheless new specimens continued to come off the production line, so the type became a familiar sight in a variety of liveries. Its increased capacity was found particularly useful at peak times on some of the trunk routes, to return seat-mile costs 27% better than a 727 of similar size or a 7% improvement over the 737-300. By the autumn of 1989 the manufacturer had sold 171 examples of the variant, of which 61 had been delivered to the customers. But not every 737 operator needed an airliner with such a capacity; a fact already appreciated by Boeing and remedied by the introduction of the Series 500.

Below:
A low pass by G-UKLA just prior to entering service.
AJW

Progress is inevitable, but it does not necessarily bring benefits for all and sundry. For many years the 737s in service had cabins designed to carry between 100 and 130 passengers depending on the duties performed. This size suited the smaller carrier admirably, so the introduction of the -300 and -400 was of academic interest to them because there was always the faithful -200. However, such complacency was ill-advised because as the newer versions grew in popularity, so production of the earlier model began to slow, until finally the long run was ended in August 1988. Fully aware that its passing would be received with dismay by some customers, it was not surprising that Boeing had already made preparations to fill the vacancy left in the ranks of the 737 family. Since the basic differences between the versions concerned the fuselage length and powerplant, one obvious solution would be to re-engine the -200 with the quieter and more efficient CFM56. Using this method the capacity remained acceptable but all the other advantages would be gained.

During its incubation period the projected design was designated the 737-1000, but as the time approached for a decision on the variant's future, Boeing changed its identity to the more logical Series 500. Prior to the formal launch on

Below:
737-500.

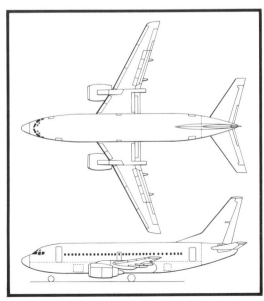

20 May 1987, the manufacturer had secured a number of customers willing to support its introduction. Amongst the leaders was the Norwegian carrier Braathens, already a long-time operator of the 737-200 and keen to replace them with the more efficient product. The company's order for 25 was almost matched by a batch of 20 for Dallas-based Southwest Airlines, although the latter also acquired options on the same number. Together with the sale of three to each of Maersk Air and Euralair — also the holder of two options — the total commitments when the go ahead was given had reached a highly satisfactory 73 aircraft.

As expected the -500 differed from its relatives in its fuselage length. Boeing had reduced it to 97ft 9in (29.8m), which was just 10in (25cm) longer than the original Series 200. Its similar size therefore enabled accommodation for between 108 and 130 passengers to be provided, the precise number depending upon the layout specified. A wide choice of electronic flightdeck instrumentation was made available to the operators so that as much commonality as possible was enjoyed by the various fleets. Although these modern devices were chosen by most clients, Southwest opted to retain the electro-mechanical variety to bring its new additions into line with its existing vast collection of 737s. Otherwise the new derivative inherited most of the -300's structure including the slightly recontoured wing, fin and tailplane extension plus the powerplant mounting. At an early stage Boeing offered the CFM56-3B1 producing 20,000lb thrust, or alternatively the derated CFM56-3B4 of 18,500lb could be substituted to meet individual requirements.

Despite the close relationship to the other family members, two years passed before the prototype -500 was rolled-out at Renton on 3 June 1989. Some four weeks later at 11.40 on 30 June, Boeing's latest creation took off for its first taste of flying under the command of Jim McRoberts, accompanied on this occasion by Ken Higgins, the company's director of flight operations. It was almost inevitable that the registration carried was N73700 because its previous custodian had recently discarded the mark in favour of a new identity. In any case, why break the tradition just when the signwriters were fully experienced with this particular combination?

A captive audience of nearly 11,000 employees witnessed the departure of the -500 as it climbed

Left:
This modern type of instrument panel is fitted to the 737-300, -400 and -500. *Boeing*

Below:
This shot of the prototype 737-500 taking off on its first flight makes an interesting comparison with the view elsewhere in the book of the -300 similarly posed. *Boeing*

Right:
With the exception of the engines, there are very few external differences between the 737-200 and -500. *Boeing*

smartly away into the somewhat unseasonal thick cloud cover at the start of its first 2hr 10min session of exploration of the Washington sky. Much of the time was taken up with the confirmation of the on-board systems and flight characteristics, but somewhat unusually a high speed test that took the aircraft to Mach 0.89 was also included. Weather conditions were not ideal so some of the planned exploits were not attempted, but the results that were attainable were very promising at such an early point in the variant's career. Sales had now reached 153 from 18 customers, most of them satisfied -200 operators.

In view of the marked similarity between the -500 and its brethren, flight testing could be restricted to proving stability and control, handling and the recalibration of the autopilot and flight-management computer. It was therefore only necessary to allocate one aircraft to the programme, compared with three and two in the case of the -300 and -400 respectively. At the conclusion of the planned 350hr or so development flying, it was expected that the FAA would award the type certification on 12 February 1990. This target did not seem unrealistic because at the end of the first month 25hr of uneventful trials had already taken place. As anticipated the timetable was maintained, to be rewarded by the receipt of the all-important piece of paper after the aircraft had spent some 375hr in the air. With the documentation complete, the way was clear for deliveries to commence towards the end of the month, with the first machine (N504SW) going to Southwest as the forerunner of the airline's 38-strong order.

Below:
Launch customer Southwest Airlines became the first to receive the 737-500. *Boeing*

7 The Military 737

Above:
The USAF acquired 19 navigation trainers which were designated T-43A. *Boeing*

Boeing designed the 737 for the civil transport market so it was something of a bonus when the type was ordered by the USAF in the early 1970s as a result of experience gained in the Vietnam war. During the course of these operations it had become apparent that there was an urgent need to increase the supply of navigators. It was a task that was currently carried out by a fleet of elderly Convair T-29s, itself a derivative of the civil Model 340/440 airliners. The replacement needed to offer greater capacity and the ability to carry more advanced equipment to improve the standard of training. Economics indicated that an off-the-shelf purchase was the most practical solution in view of the relatively small number required. After considering all the available options, the basic 737-200 airframe was chosen as being the most suitable. There was also no necessity for the Air Force to stock a vast supply of spares because all were readily available from the manufacturer as required.

Boeing therefore received an order worth some $82.4 million covering the supply of 19 specimens, all modified to meet the military specifications. A strengthened cabin floor was installed in order to cope with the heavy avionic consoles, while only nine windows were provided on each side of the fuselage. Access to the latter was restricted to two doors; one located in the traditional forward, port position with the second at the rear of the starboard side. The only other

major change visible concerned the provision of overhead sextant points in the roof of the cabin for the use of the trainee navigators. Tucked away in the rear cargo compartment was an additional fuel tank capable of carrying 800 USgal for enhanced range performance.

By now designated T-43A, the first of the latest 737 variants was rolled-out at Renton to undertake its maiden trip on 10 April 1973. Flight trials were quickly completed to the satisfaction of the FAA, so with the receipt of the type certificate, deliveries to the USAF commenced with 71-1403 on 31 July. Thereafter the remaining 18 flowed from the line at regular intervals until the last (73-1156) was taken on strength on 17 July 1974. It enabled the 57 T-29s in use to be retired with all

Below:
The trainees in the foreground can be easily monitored by one of the three instructors (centre). His seat can be moved along floor tracking to each station in turn. *USAF*

46

speed, since the newcomers were able to carry 12 navigators, four proficiency students plus three instructors. With a utilisation figure almost double that of their predecessors, the T-43As represented a considerable advance in performance and efficiency.

Initially all were allocated to the 323rd FTW based at Mather AFB, Ca, but four were later transferred to the Air National Guard, two being assigned to the Colorado ANG at Buckley near Denver, Co, for the use of navigators studying at the Air Force Academy. The other pair operated with the ANG at Andrews AFB, Md, until replaced by four C-22Bs, the designation given to some newly acquired secondhand Boeing 727s. At this point the displaced T-43As moved to Buckley to double the number of the type employed at the base. Meanwhile the bulk of the fleet has remained at Mather, although with the planned closure of this base by 1993, the 323rd FTW is due to move to Beale AFB, Ca.

During the last quarter of the 1980s it was found possible to release several T-43As for other

Above:
There are five overhead sextant ports along the cabin of the T-43A. *USAF*

Below:
This cutaway model of the T-43A shows the 19 stations used by trainees and instructors. *Boeing*

activities. In the autumn of 1988, 72-0283 was flown to Miami, Fl, for conversion into a VIP transport. This work was completed at the end of the year, so in January 1989 the aircraft was delivered to the 58th MAS based at Ramstein, West Germany. Subsequently it was regularly observed in Europe and was easily identified by its 'United States of America' livery. It was not the only example of the breed to leave the shores of its homeland because during 1987 another T-43A (72-0286) was based at Frankfurt. For the purposes of this detachment all traces of its military markings were removed and replaced by an orthodox airliner scheme. In its temporary demobbed state it adopted the civil identity N99890 for a time, but after a visit to the US it returned as N457JE. There was much speculation surrounding the movements of this machine, the most popular theory being that it was operating for the CIA.

With the exception of the USAF's order, sales of the 737 for military service have been small. In the early 1980s Boeing developed a maritime surveillance version of which three were sold to the Indonesian Air Force. Two 16ft (4.88m) long blade antennae were mounted one on each side of the upper rear fuselage to enable the high resolution, side-looking radar to function efficiently. Using

Above:
Indonesia acquired three 737 Surveillers for maritime use. Its two sideways-looking radar antennae either side of the fin are clearly seen. *Boeing*

this device it was possible to spot small ships at a range of up to 115 miles (185km) even when they were travelling in rough seas. When not required to perform in this role, the aircraft could be used for government transport work, for which purpose they were given a 14-seat first class cabin plus all-tourist accommodation for 88 passengers.

A few nations have subsequently employed the 737 for military work, but these have all been standard civil airliners rather than specially adapted versions. In recent years Boeing has had little need to seek such markets in view of the type's success amongst the airlines, but it was not

Below:
Normally the Surveiller flies at 30,000ft, but in this simulated exercise the aircraft had descended to low level to inspect a suspicious sighting on its radar. *Boeing*

always the case. In 1981 the company proposed an interesting solution to NATO's tanker shortage which would also have generated some welcome business for the manufacturer. At the time there were some 140 737s in airline service in Europe, all considered capable of modification to carry a centre-line refuelling pod. Redesignated 737-KX-150, the aircraft would have been equipped with four pallet-mounted tanks on the main deck, each containing 1,020 USgal to take the total available fuel capacity to 9,240 USgal.

If the scheme had been adopted, then the aircraft would have been ready in any emergency situation to be operated by civilian crews previously trained in the art of dispensing fuel to thirsty receivers. Boeing anticipated that one full-time squadron of 16 such 737s would be needed to provide regular refresher experience at a cost of some $276 million. Conversion and development expenses increased this figure still further until the final total reached $346 million. This alone was sufficient to ensure that the somewhat revolutionary project remained still-born.

Below:
Another military operator of the 737-200 is the Royal Thai Air Force. *Boeing*

8 Variants

Series 100

Formal design of the shorthaul airliner began on 11 May 1964, the launch customer being Lufthansa with an order for 21. Although there was a requirement for the aircraft to carry 100 seats, initially the German carrier only installed 84. The Quick Change and mixed traffic option was also offered, both versions having the large freight door in the forward fuselage. However, Boeing was unable to interest the market in the -100, so production was terminated after only 30 had been built.

Span: 93ft 0in (28.35m)
Overall length: 94ft 0in (28.65m)
Height: 37ft 0in (11.28m)
Engines: Pratt & Whitney JT8D-7 of 14,000lb (6,350kg) thrust. JT8D-9 14,500lb (6,577kg) optional
Capacity: 103.

Series 200

At an early stage Boeing recognised that a slightly larger machine would prove more attractive for airlines requiring greater capacity on short trunk routes. This led to the development of the Series 200 almost simultaneously with the -100 which it overshadowed. Subsequently the -200 Advanced became the standard model into which a number of improvements were incorporated through the years. A version with a high gross weight structure was also an option. Production ended in 1988 after 1,114 of the species had been delivered, including a number for military use. A large forward freight door was offered (-200C) for combi working, or for use on freight work when operated in its Quick Change guise (-200QC).

Span: 93ft 0in (28.35m)
Overall length: 100ft 2in (30.53m)
Height: 37ft 0in (11.28m)
Engines: Pratt & Whitney JT8D-9/9A/15/15A/17/ 17A with thrust up to 16,000lb (7,257kg) optional
Capacity: 108 to 130 depending on seat pitch and cabin layout.

Below:
The Series 200 was selling well in the early 1980s when Delta became a customer for 33 of the type. *Boeing*

Right:
Delta's sixth machine (N306DL) became the 1,000th 737 to be completed, which naturally was suitably celebrated at Renton. *Boeing*

Corporate 77-32
Developed as an executive version of the Series 200. Later the designation was changed to Corporate 200. Details as for the -200 although capacity varied according to customer requirements.

T-43A
Navigation trainer for USAF. Details as for Series 200.

Surveiller
Maritime surveillance model developed for the Indonesian Air Force. Details as for Series 200.

Capacity: 14 first class and 88 tourist class seats when used for transport duties.

Centre right:
A corporate aircraft, the 737 A6-ESH is used by the United Arab Emirates for VIP and government work.

Right:
Most of the USAF's T-43As have been based at Mather AFB, although they are due to move to Beale AFB by 1993. *Taylor/G. W. Pennick*

737-KX-150 tanker

In the early 1980s Boeing suggested that the shortage of tankers available to NATO could be overcome by the conversion of some 140 civil 737s then serving with European airlines. Details as for Series 200.

Two interesting shots of the latest three models of the 737. In the ground view the prototype Series 500 heads a -300 with the -400 bringing up the rear. The effects of the fuselage stretches are quite apparent. The airborne formation is again led by the -500, but this time KLM's -400 PH-BDT is nearest to the camera alongside N368UA, a Series 300 belonging to United. *Boeing*

737-300

Extended fuselage model powered by more efficient modern turbofans. Much commonality with the -200 was retained in the design for the benefit of operators. The -300 subsequently took over as the most popular 737 model with the airlines, which gave a renewed boost to Boeing's sales figures.

Span: 94ft 9in (28.88m)
Overall length: 109ft 7in (33.40m)
Height: 36ft 6in (11.13m)
Engines: CFM International CFM56-3B1 or -3B2 of 20,000lb (9,072kg) thrust
Capacity: 128 to 149 depending on layout specified.

Corporate 300

An executive version of the Series 300 normally equipped with about 20 seats. Otherwise details are similar to the standard airliner.

737-400

A further fuselage extension is the main feature of

Right:
Interior arrangements — mixed class.

Below left:
Interior arrangements — all tourist.

Below right:
Interior arrangements — all tourist.

this variant which also requires the services of more powerful engines.

Span: 94ft 9in (28.88m)
Overall length: 119ft 7in (36.45m)
Height: 36ft 6in (11.13m)
Engines: CFM International CFM56-3B2 of 22,000lb (9,979kg) thrust or CFM56-3C of 23,500lb (10,659kg)
Capacity: 146 to 170 depending on layout.

737-500

Designated the Series 1000 by the manufacturer when first conceived, the -500 combines the modern technology of the -300 and -400 but offers a shortened fuselage similar in length to the -200.

Span: 94ft 9in (28.88m)
Overall length: 101ft 9in (31.0m)
Height: 36ft 6in (11.13m)
Engines: CFM International CFM56-3B1 of 20,000lb (9,072kg) thrust or -3B4 of 18,500lb (8,390kg)
Capacity: 108 to 132 depending on layout.

737-1000

See Series 500.

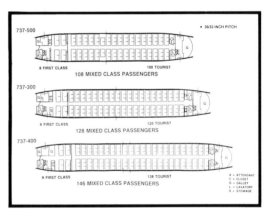

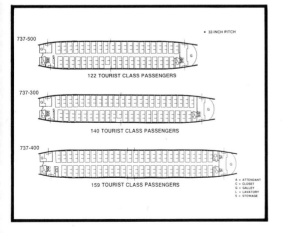

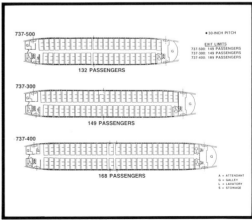

9 Mishaps

Since the 737 first entered service in February 1968 it has suffered a number of accidents. Many of these have been caused by human failings of one sort or another with no blame placed on the aircraft, but whatever the reason for the disasters, the events have generated much media coverage.

This was particularly so on 13 January 1982 when the Air Florida 737-222 N62AF crashed on take-off from Washington National. Its departure had been delayed for some 90min due to persistent snow and the need to clear the runways, but shortly before 16.30 the 737 taxied out to runway 36. Configured with 125 seats, there were only 71 passengers and five crew members on board for the scheduled trip to Tampa, Fl. Acceleration was much slower than normal and as the machine rotated towards the end of the 6,870ft strip its speed was obviously insufficient to maintain its progress. Unable to climb, the stricken 737 somehow managed to continue its nose-up journey for about one mile before striking the 14th Street bridge with its rear fuselage.

Once in the ice-covered water of the Potomac River there was little hope for the occupants, but miraculously four passengers and one stewardess survived thanks to the heroic efforts of rescuers. Because of the time and weather the bridge was carrying heavy traffic, with the result that sadly there were several drivers amongst the fatalities.

Although the 737 had been correctly de-iced during its time on the apron, it was thought that the enforced delay after passenger loading could have allowed a further coating to appear. This coupled with any slush on the runway would have caused the apparent sluggish take-off, although several other airliners departed successfully just prior to the Air Florida flight.

It had been known since 1971 that the 737 was particularly sensitive to icing, especially on the leading-edge of the wing. This was discovered when a specimen used by Boeing for test purposes developed a pitching and rolling action immediately after take-off. A number of bulletins were subsequently issued by the manufacturer advising the use of more flap and increased take-off speeds when the air temperature was below 5°C in fog, snow or freezing rain. By coincidence the CAA had produced a similarly worded order to UK operators in December, although it did not specify any change in the flap setting.

Normally control difficulties were not a problem if the icing had been dealt with properly, so pilots were reminded of the importance of this procedure. Boeing also advised against the employment of reverse thrust when taxying in freezing conditions. There was a real risk that surface moisture could be picked up and deflected on to the wing's surface before quickly reforming as ice.

Naturally a full-scale investigation was begun by the US National Transportation Safety Board (NTSB), culminating in a report issued in August 1982. It was concluded that most of the blame for the disaster was attributable to the flightdeck crew, whose experience in jet transport winter operations was very limited. The NTSB's inquiries revealed that Captain Larry Wheaton had flown only seven landings or departures in weather conditions that produced icing, while First Officer Roger Petit had only witnessed the effects on two occasions. The latter pilot was flying the 737 for take-off and apparently expressed his concern over the engines' performance during an early stage of the run, but the captain did not take the abort decision.

While this would have been preferable, the NTSB considered that a climb-out could still have been achieved successfully had the crew recognised the stall symptoms earlier. Application of more power in conjunction with the nose being lowered would then have helped the 737 to overcome the enormous handicap it was suffering from the presence of wing icing.

Although the exterior was treated by the maintenance staff while the aircraft was being turned round, the flightdeck crew did not use the engine anti-ice during the lengthy delay before departure. This omission also provoked criticism from the NTSB because the pilots should have been aware of the presence of frosting on the wing surface before attempting to take-off.

There were 11 recommendations for 737 operators in the NTSB's report including the need for all carriers to be trained in the procedure for dealing with leading edge contamination and a revision of the type's approved flight manual and check lists. Both Boeing and the FAA were advised that all modifications to the 737 and its operational technique must be completed before the next winter. It was thought that the manufacturer should have taken more positive measures to overcome the problems especially since the pitch-up tendency under the extreme conditions had been known for 10 years. Certainly the possibility of using the thermal leading edge de-icing system on the ground was in the process of being evaluated, but in the NTSB's opinion a solution should have been found more quickly.

Conditions and circumstances were completely different at Manchester on 22 August 1985 when a 737-236 operated by British Airtours suffered a catastrophic engine failure. Bound for Corfu, G-BGJL was fully laden with 131 passengers and six crew as it began its run at 06.10 along the 10,000ft runway 24. At about 125kt and some way short of rotation, a loud explosion was heard and black smoke was seen trailing from the port engine. Take-off was immediately aborted by the captain and emergency stop procedures were begun by applying both brakes and reverse thrust.

Unfortunately the latter device was a contributing factor in the swift destruction of the fuselage by the diverted flames, but at this point the crew were unaware that a fire existed, so all steps taken to bring the machine to a halt were correct. Fortuitously, as the 737 slowed a convenient taxiway allowed it to clear the runway before coming to a stop within close proximity of the airport's fire station. It was therefore possible for the tenders and rescue vehicles to be in attendance within seconds, yet 54 people died in the inferno. By chance the position of the parked aircraft had an adverse effect and allowed the relatively light 7kt wind to direct the flames around the fuselage.

Because of the fire it was not possible for the passengers to use the rear, port side door, so those seated at the back of the cabin were forced to evacuate through the two forward doors or starboard overwing exit. Most of the casualties came from the aft section although there were others unable to reach safety because of smoke and panic. Initially there was a slight delay in opening the right-hand door due to it jamming, but a second attempt by the cabin staff cleared the obstruction and the escape chute was quickly deployed.

It did not take very long for the authorities to ascertain the cause of the disaster. Failure of the number nine combustion can, caused hot gases to be directed at the outer casing's inner surface. Not intended to withstand such intense heat, a small rupture quickly increased in size with disastrous results for the 737's JT8D-15 engine. Located at the top of the power unit, this particular chamber is immediately below the integral wing fuel tank, but separated from it by the engine casing, bypass duct and lining and the substantial wing skin used at this point.

During the explosion, pieces of debris were blasted upwards with the result that several penetrated the fuel tank access panel situated just outboard of the nacelle. An 8in-diameter hole was created allowing the contents to pour through on to the hot areas of the damaged engine with immediate ignition. Despite the extremely prompt and capable attention by the fire section, the conflagration developed so rapidly that the fuselage was quickly affected as the flames spread.

Checks carried out after the event confirmed that all appropriate modifications had been done to bring the chamber up to the manufacturer's standards introduced in 1980, while it had flown 4,611hr since the last hot-section inspection and remedial repairs. Routine chamber changes were recommended at between 8,000 and 10,000hr, but often any minor cracking found during inspections at this stage could usually be easily repaired, thereby extending the service life before renewal to some 20,000hr. This goal was certainly not achieved by the errant number nine chamber carried in the 737's engine on that fateful day in August.

Within days of the tragedy the CAA issued a directive calling for the immediate inspection of JT8D engines by UK operators using both visual and isotope methods. The latter procedure was developed by British Airways and involved inserting the X-ray equipment down the hollow main shaft to photograph the chambers. Following the mass checks a number were found to be sufficiently defective to warrant engine removal. Steps were also taken to further improve the monitoring process of the JT8Ds by introducing routine checks on a cyclic basis rather than relying purely on hours-flown.

Obviously too late for those lost in the disaster, at least the event inspired a number of changes designed to improve safety for future travellers. Although some of the CAA's new regulations were already pending at the time of the Manchester accident, a greater sense of urgency was apparent when the effective date of introduction was advanced. While there was no requirement to alter the emergency exits themselves, access to them needed to be improved. Airlines had two choices by which to meet the directive. The seat pitch of the row immediately adjacent to the hatches could be increased to give more space, or alternatively the seat alongside the wall on both sides of the cabin could be removed altogether.

Not only would this provide more room for departing passengers, but the opening of the emergency hatch would be made easier for the passenger occupying the seat next to the exit. Previously this was not always simple in a 130-seat configured 737, especially since the panel weighed 50lb. Readjusting the interiors was expected to bring extra costs to the carriers, although in reality the changes were effected without undue loss of capacity.

Even before the Manchester accident the CAA intended to introduce floor-level emergency escape path lighting to assist passengers when the cabin was filled with dense smoke as in the Manchester case. As a direct result, the implementation date was brought forward to 1 December 1987. A similar advance was made with the enforcement of the requirement for fire-resistant seats, although the latter was made possible by the progress in the production of fire-blocking materials.

When the Air Accidents Investigation Branch (AAIB) report was released several years later, it made 31 recommendations. In addition to many already implemented by the CAA, it considered that on-board water spray fire-extinguishing systems should be developed for commercial airliners as soon as possible. The AAIB also urged the authorities to pursue the provision of smokehoods or masks to give passengers some protection when toxic fumes were present. While several manufacturers were testing such items, the widespread introduction was unlikely in the foreseeable future especially if the cabin spray systems were approved.

Neither ice nor fire brought near disaster to the Aloha Airlines 737-297 N73711 on 28 April 1988. It had departed from Hilo, Hi, at 14.00 on the routine inter-island service AQ243 and was scheduled to land at Honolulu 40min later. When it was well into the flight at an altitude of 24,000ft, the crew suddenly declared an emergency situation and indicated that the machine had suffered a rapid decompression. At the time it was passing some 15 miles south of Maui Island, the nearest point to which the 737 could divert.

Prior to its landing no one could have envisaged the scale of the damage which was reminiscent of a shot-up B-17 limping home from a raid in World War 2. A substantial portion of the upper fuselage from a point just aft of the forward entrance door to the leading edge of the wing had been lost. This included the removal of the side walls down to floor level which left the passenger seats in the cabin clearly visible. It was truly miraculous that the crew managed to bring the mutilated 737 back for a safe landing and the opportunity for immediate investigation. Of the 95 people on board before the accident, it was equally amazing that only one — a stewardess — was lost, although several of the passengers suffered serious injuries from flying debris and the effects of the wind.

Representatives of the NTSB were quickly on the scene to seek the cause of the failure, which could possibly affect other 737s. In fact N73711 had flown some 35,000hr during the course of

89,193 flights since it was the 152nd of its type off the Boeing line in 1969. This record made it the second highest flight-cycle 737 in the world, beaten only by another machine in the Aloha fleet. Since much of the airline's work involves frequent short-sector inter-island links, its aircraft are naturally subjected to an abnormally high number of take-offs, landings and pressurisation sequences.

Originally Boeing had set a 75,000-cycle economic design life on the type, but the manufacturer had subsequently subjected a test specimen to 130,000 sequences in 1987, considerably more than that of the Aloha machine. Nonetheless the company had been in contact with the Hawaii-based carrier concerning the condition of its ageing 737s. Several visits were made during the autumn of 1987 at a time when two of the three oldest machines were undergoing major inspections. When N73712 was checked it was apparent that corrosion existed around lap splices and the belly skin of the fuselage. There were also a number of cracks and missing fastener heads found in the vicinity of the door and access panel cut-outs. Its close relative (N73713) had less damage to the body, but in this case some corrosion existed on the wing spars.

Undoubtedly the very nature of Aloha's operations in a highly corrosive environment contributed in no small way to the condition of the 737s examined. Boeing therefore submitted a series of recommendations to the airline so that permanent repairs to the high-cycle aircraft could be carried out by the spring of 1988, but after due consideration Aloha decided to defer this step until the end of the year. Somewhat concerned by this proposal, the manufacturer despatched its engineers back to Hawaii in order to emphasise the urgency for the thorough overhaul. Two weeks later N73711 acquired an open-top.

After the event Aloha stated that it had been assured by Boeing that it was safe to continue flying its high-cycle 737s. This was quickly denied by the manufacturer by pointing out that it would never make such a promise without first conducting a full inspection. Prior to 1984 Aloha did pursue a corrosion-control programme, but this was replaced by routine checks in that year. After the 1988 incident the airline reintroduced the procedure and added other improvements in quality control. To its credit the surviving trio of elderly aircraft (N73711/12/13) were voluntarily grounded to be broken up for spares in July.

Ultimately the NTSB report blamed Aloha for its failure to detect the fatigue damage and for its inadequate maintenance policy. The FAA was also included in the criticisms because it should have noted this weakness and made the inspection of all 737 lap joints compulsory as recommended by Boeing. While lessons were learned from this regrettable affair, it was not the first time that corrosion had been responsible for a 737's demise, unhappily with a far greater number of fatalities.

On 5 August 1981 a Far Eastern Air Transport specimen registered B-2603 was operating a scheduled service from Taipei when cabin pressure was lost at 20,000ft. After descending to 10,000ft and ascertaining that there was no obvious damage, the journey was completed as planned. Just over two weeks later on 22 August, the same aircraft suffered a similar problem 10min after a morning departure from Taipei for a return sortie to the Pescadores Islands. On this occasion the crew elected to return to base for repairs, which were duly completed in time for B-2603 to take over the domestic run to the southern Taiwan port of Kaohsiung later in the day.

When some 60 miles south of the capital with 104 passengers and six crew on board, the aircraft suffered a major structural failure at 22,000ft before crashing in hilly countryside. At first the Taiwanese authorities thought that sabotage was a likely cause but this was soon ruled out. Significantly the machine was number 151 on the Boeing production line in 1969 and therefore the immediate neighbour of the Aloha specimen. Careful study of the wreckage produced the conclusion that serious belly corrosion was evident although this alone was not thought to be the cause of the crash. Nevertheless, towards the end of the year the FAA issued a directive to all operators of the first 418 737s built. It called for an inspection to be carried out for signs of damage to the aircrafts' interior underbody skin. Production of subsequent airframes differed because Boeing changed its manufacturing technique from stiffening with bonded doublers to a process by which the necessary skin cross-section was chemically milled.

Indian Airlines was one carrier which carried out the checks following the FEAT crash and as a result found that a considerable amount of corrosion was present around the bottom of the rear pressure bulkhead. A crack at the web joint in this component was responsible for VT-EAJ experiencing total depressurisation on 12 October 1982 while flying on the Bombay-Goa route. Fortunately the aircraft was able to land without any further trouble. Severe corrosion was rife in other parts of the structure, much of it not accessible during normal routine maintenance. It was only located after under-fuselage panels had been removed during the intensive investigation.

Unlike the earlier 737s, the Series 400 was destined to undergo a number of setbacks soon after its introduction into service in 1988. In early November, British Midland had leased two of the variants for use on its domestic trunk routes. Consequently G-OBME found itself operating the airline's flight BD092 from Heathrow to Belfast on 8 January 1989 with 117 passengers and eight crew on board. When about 10min or so into the flight, the crew reported that excessive vibration was being experienced accompanied by a fire warning from the starboard engine, which was then successfully shut down. Since everything appeared to be under control, the captain opted to divert to the company's home base at East Midlands rather than the slightly nearer Luton or Birmingham.

As the aircraft was cleared for its descent and approach there was no reason to suppose that the single-engine landing would not be completely straightforward. However, as the 737 headed for runway 27 the pilot reported that the second CFM56 was now giving trouble, which was forcing the machine well below the normal level. Somehow he managed to coax the sinking airliner over the village of Kegworth — which lies about two miles to the east of the airport — but was unable to reach the threshold of the runway before the stalling 737 made contact with the ground. It fell nose-high into a cutting containing the M1 motorway, causing the tail section to bend upwards as the doomed jet slid across the carriageway before coming to rest in three main pieces on the opposite bank.

Providentially at this instant there was a gap in the normally dense traffc flow so at least no vehicles were involved in the disaster. Rescue workers were quickly on the scene having anticipated the outcome after observing the 737's excessive loss of height in the final stages of its flight. Mercifully there was no fire, although leaking fuel constituted a real risk at first. Nevertheless 44 people lost their lives as a result of the crash of a brand new airliner which had only 518hr in its log book.

Investigations were concentrated on the two CFM56s and the instrument wiring, because survivors' statements referred to evidence of a fire in the port engine yet it was the starboard unit that the crew had shut down. The BMA machine was equipped with two of the more powerful 23,500lb thrust CFM56-C3s, whereas others of the breed employed the 22,000lb -3B2 model which is also fitted to the 737-300. Once removed from the wreck they were despatched to the SNECMA assembly plant in France for a complete strip-down and scrutiny.

Even before these checks, preliminary inspections soon revealed that the port engine had suffered severe fan blade damage with obvious indications of having been on fire, whereas no such signs were apparent in the starboard CFM56. Crossed wiring was a distinct possibility and would explain the reason for the strange actions. Checks were ordered on all 737-300s and -400s worldwide, but no errors were found in the wiring responsible for the fire warning or engine vibration displays on the flightdeck.

Although grounded for a short time, in the absence of any positive proof of malfunction, the 737s returned to service upon completion of the examinations. Some months later the CFM56-3C again gave grounds for concern when, in two separate incidents, engines powering 737-400s suffered fan blade failures. The first instance involved Dan-Air's G-BNNL which was in the late stages of its climb out of Gatwick en route to Menorca. Similar circumstances prevailed two days later when British Midland's G-OBMG was flying the Heathrow-Belfast sector. In this case the damaged engine was shut down followed by a safe diversion to East Midlands, but undoubtedly it was a traumatic experience for both passengers and crew.

No time was lost by the CAA in grounding all CFM56-3C-powered 737s on 12 June, a move copied by both Boeing and the engine manufacturer during the next day. The latter was confident that the cause of the failures was due to the demand for increased power from the variant which was almost identical to the lower-powered -3B. The extra 1,500lb thrust was achieved by different fuelling and higher rotational speeds, both creating additional stress on the fan. At the end of the month the ban on flying the Series 400s was lifted subject to the blades and discs having been replaced and the engine derated to the well-proven and trouble-free -3B standard of 22,000lb. With these modifications completed, the operators quickly returned their machines to service while CFM went on with research to find a permanent remedy.

Eventually the BMA crash produced a number of safety suggestions aimed at preventing a similar occurrence in the future. They included an external video monitor so that the crew could observe any airframe malfunction and a review of instrument panel design to avoid the risk of confusion. It was also considered essential that training sessions should emphasise the high accuracy and reliability levels of the new electronic devices. In addition reference was made to the procedures for communications between the flight deck and cabin staff, because although the latter were aware of the engine fire, they assumed that the pilots were aware of the situation.

On 20 September the 737-400 was once again the subject of much attention by the media when one of USAir's fleet crashed on take-off from New York's La Guardia airport. Conditions were not good as N416US began its run in darkness along the 7,000ft runway at the start of its scheduled trip to Charlotte, NC. Although only light rain was falling, earlier heavy downpours had left the strip covered with water which was thought to have been the probable reason for the aircraft's sluggish behaviour. Whatever the cause, before reaching the point of rotation the crew decided to abort the departure, but were unable to stop the forward progress before the 737 slid off into the East River.

This action broke the fuselage into three sections, with the nose firmly wedged on to a wood and concrete pier used for mounting runway lights. Within a very short time rescuers were on the scene to assist those in the water, their prompt action no doubt responsible for the fact that only two passengers were lost from the total of 61 occupants on board. During the ensuing investigation the NTSB found there was little evidence of any failure revealed by the flight recorders, although there were minor rudder deviations consistent with skid marks found on the runway. Investigations were therefore centred on the tail trim system which could either have been mis-set by the pilot or possess a basic design fault.

It transpired that neither of the flightdeck crew had much experience with the 737-400 especially in the prevailing weather conditions. The Captain had only accumulated 136hr on the type, but it was the First Officer's first operational sortie. While not the ideal combination of expertise, the FAA began looking into the desirability of modifications to the implicated trim switch. A ruling that the rim of the aft control console should be raised was issued, at the same time stipulating that the shape of the actual knob should be changed. Previously the switch had been known to stick instead of self-centring as intended, a habit which adversely affected the rudder trim. Because of its mounting position, there was also a distinct danger that it could be moved by a misplaced foot belonging to an observer on the jump-seat.

When the NTSB report on the accident was eventually published nine months later, it found the cause to have been pilot error. It was critical of the captain's failure to exercise his command authority during the take-off and also his attempts to correct the aircraft's drift by nosewheel steering. In addition the autobrake was not used which delayed effective braking, while the first officer had inadvertently disconnected the autothrottle thereby lengthening the ground run. Neither crew members was monitoring airspeed which led to the captain aborting the flight 5kt above that computed for lift-off. Although the rudder was mistrimmed to give a 16° deflection it remained undetected to produce the ultimate result. Since the incident, Boeing has modified the type's trim system to prevent a repetition.

Problems with engines has not been confined to the spate of incidents involving the CFM56, because on other occasions it was the JT8D that made the news. On 5 December 1987 a USAir 737-200 had reached about 5,000ft after take-off from Philadelphia when the pilot reported that there had been a loss of power from the starboard engine. This was not surprising because the aircraft had shed the entire unit without the knowledge of the crew. While the unplanned solo flight of the jet missile ended abruptly in a field near Deptford Township, NJ, the aircraft returned to its starting point to land without problems and no casualties.

A defective mounting bolt was found to have been the cause of the loss, so the FAA issued a directive that ultrasonic inspection must henceforth be carried out on the item after every 600 landings. This was thought adequate in view of the rarity of the event and the fact that a back-up cable support had been recommended in 1982. Nonetheless the latter device had not served its intended purpose very efficiently, so in September 1988 the FAA instructed operators to provide an improved secondary support system within 4,000 landings.

All was well until 20 January 1989 when another 737-200 decided to dispense with its starboard JT8D after take-off from Chicago O'Hare. Again much to the credit of the aircraft and crew, Piedmont's N242US managed to return to the airport without further ado with none of the 33 occupants injured.

An emergency instruction was immediately issued to halve the interval allowed between inspections of the engine mounting bolts common to the 737-100 and -200. This meant that the ultrasonic testing now had to be carried out every 300 landings, but since the Piedmont aircraft had only completed 35 since its last check, the value of the examinations seemed questionable. All three bolts had fractured, although it was the rear example which has set the process in motion because the reason for its failure was fatigue. This left the remaining pair and the back-up cable unsuccessfully to carry the weight of the entire unit, since N242US had yet to acquire its new support structure.

When the JT8D abandoned the 737 it had some 1,300ft to fall before landing on open land near to the airport perimeter, fortunately without casualties. Understandably there was some concern expressed by those on the ground who did not appreciate these random attacks by wayward jet engines.

Far more incidents in varying degrees of seriousness have been due to take-offs, landings and approaches. In India collisions with wandering bulls on runways has not been unknown, with dire consequences for all concerned. A snowblower on the runway caused the crash of Pacific Western's C-FPWC as it attempted to land in a blinding snowstorm at Cranbrook, BC, on 11 February 1978.

In more recent times a completely unnecessary accident involved the Varig Series 200 PP-VMK. On 3 September 1989 it left Marabá with flight RG254 bound for Belém on Brazil's northern coast. There were 48 passengers and six crew on board for the trip which was scheduled to take 1hr, but it never arrived at its destination. Instead the crew was forced to make a landing in the dense Amazon rain forest when the fuel was exhausted. Apparently the pilot set a heading of 270° instead of the correct 027° so the airliner finished its journey some 600 miles off course. While navigation does not seem to have been a strong point, at least some skill was displayed in the landing survived by 41 of the occupants.

Ground security checks have been tightened to such an extent that it should be impossible for bombs to be secreted on board airliners, but it was thought that such a device could have been responsible for the explosion suffered by the Philippines Airlines Series 300 EI-BZG on 11 May 1990. The incident occurred at Manila shortly after push-back, resulting in the death of eight people and serious injuries to a further 30. Naturally the first reaction was to suspect sabotage, but investigators began to turn their attention to a possible fault on the aircraft. By the end of July a defective fuel tank float switch and wiring were considered to be the likely culprits, so the NTSB recommended that the FAA should issue a Directive to all operators calling for an immediate check of the appropriate components on all Series 300s, 400s and 500s.

Items that required inspection included the fuel boost pump, float switch and wiring looms since signs of chafing and rubbing had been found. After delivery the airline's engineers had installed logo lights on the eight-month old machine, a task which involved additional wire to be passed through vapour seals. It was thought that a mixture of fuel and air could have been ignited due to arcing from worn insulation. Surprisingly the Authority decided against taking any action until more definite evidence was forthcoming to confirm the suspicions. Undoubtedly many operators subsequently carried out the checks on a voluntary basis, but no further instances were reported.

Many of the mishaps have clearly illustrated the robustness of the 737.

Appendix 1. Customer Numbers

At an early stage Boeing devised a system of customer codes for identification purposes. This was achieved by allocating the second two digits of the three figure series indicator to individual airlines. In this way Lufthansa's 737 Series 100s, 200s, 300s and 500s became 130s, 230s, 330s and 530s. Similarly 48 was reserved for Aer Lingus, so its Series 200s were known as -248s and the later variants became -348s, -448s and -548s. These identities are retained throughout the aircraft's life and are also applied in the same manner to other types such as the 727, 747 etc. When Boeing had used all 100 number combinations, the company began a new batch in the range A0 to A9, B0 to B9 etc, followed by 0A to 9A, 0B to 9B and so on. All were similarly issued as before.

01	Piedmont Airlines	93	Pacific Airlines/Air Cal	N3	Brazilian Air Force
02	Wien Consolidated	96	Quebecair	N8	Yemen Airways
04	Britannia Airways	97	Aloha Airlines	N9	Niger Government
05	Braathens	98	Air Zaire	P5	Thai Airways
06	KLM	A1	VASP	P6	Gulf Air
09	China Airlines	A3	PLUNA	Q2	Air Gabon
10	Northern Consolidated	A4	Air Cal	Q3	Southwest Airlines Japan
12	Malaysian-Singapore	A8	Indian Airlines	Q5	Air Liberia
14	Pacific Southwest	A9	Transair	Q8	International Lease Finance
17	CP Air	B1	DETA Mozambique		Corpn
19	New Zealand National	B2	Air Madagascar	R4	Alyemda
	/Air New Zealand	B3	Aeromaritime	R8	Air Tanzania
22	United Air Lines	B6	Royal Air Maroc	S2	Federal Express
23	American Airlines	B7	USAir	S3	Air Europe
24	Continental Airlines	C3	Cruzeiro do Sul	T0	Texas Air
28	Air France	C9	Luxair	T4	Air Florida/CAAC
29	Sabena	D6	Air Algerie	T5	Orion Airways
30	Lufthansa	E1	Eastern Provincial	T7	Monarch Airlines
32	Delta Airlines	E3	LADECO	U9	Polynesian Airlines
36	British Airways	E7	Arkia	V5	Bahamasair
40	Pakistan International	F9	Nigeria Airways	W0	Yunnan Provincial
41	Varig	G7	America West Airlines	W6	Government of Morocco
42	Nordair	H3	Tunis Air	X2	Air Pacific
44	South African Airways	H4	Southwest Airlines	X4	Supair
47	Western Airlines	H6	Malaysian Airline System	X6	Markair
48	Aer Lingus	H7	Cameroon Airlines	X9	Indonesian Air Force
58	El Al	H9	Jugoslav Airlines	Y0	GPA Group
59	Avianca	J6	CAAC	Y5	Air Malta
60	Ethiopian Airways	J8	Sudan Airways	Z6	Royal Thai Air Force
66	Egyptair	K2	Transavia	Z8	South Korean Air Force
68	Saudia	K3	Aviogenex	Z9	Lauda Air
69	Kuwait Airways	K5	Hapag-Lloyd	2C	Air UK Leisure
70	Iraqi Airways	K6	SAHSA	3A	Nordstress
75	Pacific Western	K9	Bavaria Flug	5A	Midway Airlines
76	Australian Airlines	L7	Air Nauru	5B	Germania
77	Ansett	L9	Maersk Air	5C	Xiamen Airlines
81	All Nippon	M2	TAAG Angola	6B	Novair International
82	TAP-Air Portugal	M6	Royal Brunei Airlines	7A	Far East Air Transport
84	Olympic Airways	M8	Trans European Airways	9A	ARAVCO
86	Iran Air	M9	Zambia Airways	9D	Linjeflyg
87	Aerolineas Argentinas	N0	Air Zimbabwe		
91	Frontier Airlines	N1	Venezuelan Air Force		

Many of the airlines which have employed the 737 at some time or other in the type's career are included in this section.

Abelag   *Belgium*
(*See* Air Belgium)

Aer Lingus   *Eire*
First introduced by the airline in 1969, the 737 fleet has subsequently seen service on most routes. Four of the -200s were acquired as combis and in recent years have been used for night freight work in addition to normal passenger duties. Two -300s were delivered in late 1987 specifically for use on the busy London-Dublin sector, while a similar number of -400s arrived two years later. During 1990 Aer Lingus was expected to receive some of its five -500s on order.

Aerolineas Argentinas   *Argentina*
In 1970 the airline took delivery of six 737-200s with five more added by 1974. Of these one was damaged beyond repair in September 1988, but otherwise the fleet remains unchanged. Transavia has leased a 737 to the airline on several short periods during the years.

Aeromaritime   *France*
Although operating as a UTA subsidiary since 1966, it was not until 1988 that the airline began passenger charter work with a number of leased 737-300s (F-GFUA/H) carrying the company's own livery.

Aerotour   *France*
After operations began in 1976, passenger charters were flown using a fleet of Caravelles. In April 1980 a pair of ex-Maersk 737-200s were leased from GPA to start a programme of re-equipment, but on 5 November the company ended its career, so two days later the aircraft (F-GCGR/S) returned to the lessor.

Air Algerie   *Algeria*
The carrier's first 737-200 was delivered in 1971 to mark the beginning of a 16-strong fleet by 1983. There have been no losses although the original machine (7T-VEC) was sold to Air Mali in 1982. Following the demise of Air Florida, three of the latter's orders were transferred to Air Algerie as Model 2T4s instead of the airline's usual 2D6s.

Air Atlantis   *Portugal*
Operations by this Air Portugal subsidiary began in mid-1985 using aircraft transferred from the parent company. Subsequently the airline acquired its own 737-200s for use on passenger charters throughout Europe, while the first of four -300s leased from Bavaria joined the fleet during 1989.

Air Belgium   *Belgium*
Formed 1979 as Abelag Airways, it was not long before the company adopted the present title. A number of 737s have been employed through the

Below:
Seen here on passenger duties, EI-ASC was delivered to Aer Lingus in 1969 as a convertible. It was adapted for all-cargo work in January 1990. *AJW*

years mainly for IT charter work on behalf of the Belgian travel industry, although the airline is to be found at many other centres in Europe. All the 737s that have been operated in the past have been leased, although rarely have there been more than two in service at any one time. During 1989 a -400 (OO-ILH) replaced the earlier versions in use.

Air Berlin   *USA*
April 1979 marked the start of operations, with a trip from Berlin (Tegel) to Palma. For the first few years a varied collection of 707s and 737s were employed from time to time, but in 1982 a 737-200 was leased from Hapag-Lloyd (D-AHLD) which, with the new identity N2941W, thereafter handled all the carrier's charter business to the Mediterranean, Canaries and Madeira. After four years with the company, the aircraft was replaced by the Series 300 N67AB in April 1986, this time leased from GPA. It was therefore a logical step for the company when it acquired the Series 400 N11AB in 1990.

Air California (Air Cal)   *USA*
Scheduled services were commenced in January 1967 when several routes were flown within California. In 1981 the shortened version of its title was adopted by which time a large fleet of 737-200s had been assembled to cope with the much expanded network along the American west coast. In 1985 the first of the Series 300s

Below:
Air Algerie has operated the 737-200 7T-VEQ since 1976. *G. W. Pennick*

arrived, but the order was not completed before the airline was purchased by American Airlines in June 1987 with the inevitable loss of identity. All the aircraft were then absorbed into the latter's fleet or transferred to other subsidiaries.

Air Charter International   *France*
Formed in 1966 by Air France, Air Charter undertakes charter services from a large number of French airports for its parent company, Caravelles and Boeing 727s were used for many years, but in the mid-1980s 737-200s began to appear in ACI livery, although operated on its behalf by airlines such as Europe Aero Service and Euralair. Two ex-Hapag-Lloyd machines were bought by the carrier in 1988 to become F-GFLV and F-GFLX.

Air Comores   *Comoro Islands*
Formed in 1975, the airline employed one 737-200 for its limited scheduled services in 1985. Registered D2-CAJ, the aircraft was leased from South African Airways for about one year before reverting to its normal identity of ZS-CIB upon its return.

Air Djibouti   *Djibouti*
Several 737s have been leased from Sabena for short periods, but the airline normally operates a DC-9 for its scheduled network.

Air Europa   *Spain*
Created in 1986, Air Europa operates a large number of IT charter flights from airports throughout Europe to the Mediterranean and the Canaries. It is closely associated with Air Europe

Above:
In the mid-1980s Air Berlin employed N2941W, a 737-200 leased from Hapag-Lloyd. *G. W. Pennick*

which enables frequent exchanges of aircraft to be made between the two fleets of 737-300s.

Air Europe   *United Kingdom*
Charter operations began with 737-200s in May 1979, which soon found themselves shuttling backwards and forwards between Gatwick and the Mediterranean centres. A useful exchange agreement was reached with Air Florida in the early 1980s whereupon several of each carrier's aircraft crossed the Atlantic to assist in peak periods. Following the US airline's demise, Air Europe found some alternative employment with British Airtours for the aircraft made surplus due to falling demand. The first scheduled route licences were secured in 1985 which marked the start of an impressive network in Europe. In 1987 the older 737s were finally replaced by Series 300s, while 1989 saw the arrival of the first of the larger -400s for use on both charter and scheduled work. There are frequent interchanges of aircraft between Air Europa and Norway Airlines (Air Europe Scandinavia).

Air Europe Scandinavia   *Norway*
(*See* Norway Airlines)

Air Florida   *USA*
A number of scheduled services were begun by Air Florida in September 1972, all linking various airports within its home state. For more than five years the carrier just avoided the need to wind up its affairs, but in 1977 the company was reorganised with startling results. From that point it expanded beyond all recognition to become America's fastest growing airline. The 737 was chosen as the standard equipment and it was this type which was largely responsible for the success rate. Then just as suddenly fortunes changed, with Air Florida's meteoric rise abruptly transformed into a desperate but unsuccessful struggle for survival in 1984.

Air France   *France*
Although the airline considered the 737 well suited to its needs, due to staff opposition it was not until the end of 1982 that the first of a 12-strong order was delivered. Another seven joined the fleet in due course, the entire batch being Series 200s. Commencing in 1991, Air France is expected to receive 12 Series 500s.

Air Gabon   *Gabon*
A single 737-200 combi version has been operated by Air Gabon since 1978. Registered TR-LXL, the aircraft is used on the carrier's services within Africa.

Above:
Air Florida rapidly built up a large fleet of 737s, N58AF being delivered in 1980. *AJW*

Air Guinee   *Guinea*

A number of scheduled routes are flown by the flag carrier's solitary 737. Registered 3X-GCB, the combi was delivered in 1981, and has since maintained the links with neighbouring states in Africa.

Air Lanka   *Sri Lanka*

A 737 has been used by the airline since 1979, although the individual specimen changed occasionally as leases expired. In June 1985 the airline acquired its own machine which became 4R-ULH prior to entering service on the carrier's routes to India and other points.

Air Liberia   *Liberia*

The only 737 operated by this company was the combi EL-AIL between June 1978 and September 1982, when it was employed on the airline's international routes. When these were cut back the aircraft was no longer needed so it was sold to Lina Congo as TN-AEE.

Air Madagascar   *Madagascar*

In 1969 a 737-200 (5R-MFA) was delivered to the airline for use on its range of regional and domestic services. At the end of 1972 a second joined the fleet to become 5R-MFB; the pair then serving together until the present day.

Air Mali   *Mali*

When in need of a 737 for its regional services, Air Mali acquired 7T-VEC from Air Algerie in 1982. Wearing its new identity TZ-ADL, the aircraft was used on the scheduled routes until 1986 when it was leased as G-BMMZ to Britannia Airways. There was no hurry for it to return because in 1988 Air Mali ceased its activities.

Above:
Schedules and charters became the duties for Air Malta's 737-200s, 9H-ABB being the second to be delivered in March 1983. *AJW*

Air Malta   *Malta*

Re-equipment began in 1983 when the first of three new 737-200s arrived to gradually take over from the ageing 720s. By 1988 the fleet contained six of the type which then took over the responsibility for both schedules and charter flights to numerous points in Europe and Africa. Three 737-500s are on order for delivery in 1993.

Air Nauru   *Nauru*

This Pacific island is linked to neighbouring countries such as Australia, New Zealand and Hong Kong plus other islands in the vicinity by Air Nauru's three 737s acquired in 1975, 1978 and 1982 registered C2-RN3, C2-RN6, and C2-RN8 respectively. A fourth (C2-RN9) joined the airline in 1983, but was sold two years later.

Air New Zealand   *New Zealand*

Prior to 1978 it was New Zealand Airways that operated domestic services with a fleet that included eight 737-200s. On 1 April this carrier was merged with the international airline, Air New Zealand, to operate under the latter name.

Top:
First to be delivered to Air New Zealand after the merger with NAC was the Series 200, ZK-NAR.
Boeing

Above:
Air Pacific's solitary 737-200, DQ-FDM. *Boeing*

Accordingly the 737s were transferred, although in due course some of the older machines were sold and replaced by others of their kind.

Air Nippon   Japan
(*See* Nihon Kinkyori Airways)

Air Pacific   Fiji
One 737-200 (DQ-FDM) has been operated by the airline for its regional services since October 1981.

Air Portugal   Portugal
A re-equipment programme brought seven new 737-200s to the Air Portugal fleet in 1983, joined two years later by a pair of secondhand specimens from Condor. The newcomers were used on various European scheduled routes and also for charter work with Air Atlantis. Five Series 300s were ordered for deliveries to be completed in 1990.

Airsul   Portugal
Created in 1989 for charter work, this Portuguese carrier began with a 737-200 leased from Britannia but was due to receive a pair of other Series 200s in 1990.

Air Tanzania   Tanzania
Two Series 200 combis (5H-MFA/B) were delivered to the carrier in late 1978/early 1979 for use on the growing number of international services operated from Dar-es-Salaam.

Air UK Leisure   United Kingdom
Launched in April 1988, the airline became the first European operator of the 737-400 when it took delivery of G-UKLA in October. By the end of 1989 three of the type were on strength with others due for delivery between 1990 and 1992.

Air Zaire   Zaire
Regional schedules were begun with the delivery of three 737-200s (9Q-CNI, 9Q-CNJ and 9Q-CNK) in 1973/74. Another (9Q-CNL) was operated on a year-long lease starting in 1976, but this was duly returned. In 1984 the airline lost the services of 9Q-CNJ when it was severely damaged, but it was not replaced.

Air Zimbabwe   Zimbabwe
The company introduced a 737-200 on to its regional services in 1985 when OY-APS was leased from Maersk. Deliveries of Air Zimbabwe's own three machines began in 1986 with Z-WPA, which was quickly followed in the New Year by -WPB and -WPC. It allowed the return of the Danish example, and thereafter the fleet has not changed in size.

Air 2000   United Kingdom
Until January 1989, Air 2000 was exclusively a 757 operator. However, the airline then leased a 737-300 (G-KKUH) to use for IT charter flights which did not support the larger capacity airliner.

Airways International Cymru
United Kingdom
In March 1985 the airline bought the 737-200 G-BAZI to supplement its One-Elevens on IT charters. Two years later the Series 300 G-BNCT was leased for similar activities, but in early 1988 it returned to the lessor due to the cessation of operations by Airways Cymru.

Alaska Airlines   _USA_
Seven 737-200Cs are used by the carrier for some of its extensive network of services along the American West Coast.

All Nippon   _Japan_
Since taking delivery of its first 737-200 in 1969, All Nippon has used the type for its vast domestic and regional services. Although the older machines were replaced by new arrivals in the 1970s, the fleet has remained fairly constant in size with no additions since 1979.

Aloha Airlines   _USA_
Aloha's 737-200s have been used on the frequent Hawaiian inter-island shuttle services since the early 1970s. Due to these short sectors the airline's aircraft feature amongst those that have completed the highest number of cycles. After an

Below:
Alaska Airlines took delivery of the 737-200 combi N730AS in 1981. _Boeing_

accident in 1988 the oldest members of the fleet were retired and replaced by a pair of Series 300s (N301AL/2AL). A further four are due to join the fleet, while Aloha also holds options on a similar quantity.

Alyemda   *Yemen*
One 737-200 (4W-ABZ) has been used by the airline since the aircraft was delivered in 1976. It is normally employed on services linking Aden with neighbouring States in the Gulf and Middle East.

Amberair   *United Kingdom*
After the collapse of Airways International Cymru, an attempt was made to replace the lost capacity by forming Amberair at Cardiff. Operations began in April 1988 with a programme of IT flights using a pair of 737-200s (G-BKMS and G-BOSA), the latter having previously been G-BAZI with Airways Cymru. However, in November, Amberair was taken over by Paramount Airways which in turn was forced to cease operations in August 1989. During the early part of 1990 there were signs that Amberair might be restarted, although the state of the travel market did not encourage such a move.

American Airlines   *USA*
Until American acquired Air Cal in July 1987 the airline had no 737s in its vast fleet. Most of the aircraft so gained were re-registered with an 'AA' suffix as customary and prepared for lease to Braniff.

America West   *USA*
It was only in August 1983 when America began scheduled services from its base at Phoenix, Az,

using four secondhand 737-200s. As in the case of Air Florida, America West's rise was spectacular until at the end of 1989 it was considered to be one of America's major carriers. In the meantime the 737 fleet was expanded to over 70 assorted specimens obtained from various sources. While the majority are Series 200s, one -100 (N708AW) is also employed together with a growing number of -300s.

Ansett Airlines   *Australia*
The airline operates a young 16-strong fleet of 737-300s on its network of domestic schedules. These aircraft replaced a dozen five-year-old Series 200s, which were sold to America West in 1986.

Ansett New Zealand   *New Zealand*
Three of the first five 737s built helped to maintain the carrier's domestic scheduled services from mid-1987. Originally Series 100s with Lufthansa, they subsequently joined America West before transferring to New Zealand. The fleet also includes an ex-Singapore Series 100 and one -200 of 1969 vintage, but the one-time German machines were for sale in 1990.

Arkia   *Israel*
Two 737-200s (4X-BAB/C) were received by Arkia in 1983, but in the following year they were sold. Thereafter the carrier leased a 737 from the parent company for use on passenger charters when required.

Asiana Airlines   *South Korea*
Initially only domestic schedules and charter services were flown by this carrier after oper-

ations began in December 1988, but international sectors were due to be introduced with the delivery of additional 737-400s and a pair of 767s. Eight of the former were in service by early 1990.

Atlanta Icelandic   *Iceland*
Formed in February 1986, the airline intended to offer passenger and freight charters. One 737-200 was leased by the company as TF-ABJ in January 1989 to almost immediately begin regular cargo work for Finnair.

Australian Airlines   *Australia*
Known as Trans Australian Airways until 1986, the change of name also marked the point when delivery of 16 737-300s began. These had all entered service by the end of 1989 whereupon the first of nine Series 400s joined the fleet, the final member of the batch being due in 1991.

Avianca   *Colombia*
A pair of Series 100s were bought by Avianca and duly delivered in November 1968. After some three years on the domestic routes, both were sold to the Luftwaffe and although flown to Germany, the 737s were resold to Boeing before entering service. Thereafter Avianca had no further involvement with the type.

Aviogenex   *Yugoslavia*
Formed in 1968 with the intention of operating passenger charters to Yugoslavia from various points in Europe, for many years Aviogenex depended upon Tu-134s for its activities. Later 727s were added to the fleet, and in 1987 the first of two new 737-200s arrived. Other examples have subsequently been leased for the peak seasons as required.

Bahamasair   *Bahamas*
Scheduled passenger and freight services are operated with four 737-200s (C6-BEH, -BEQ, -BEX and -BFC), although these have been supplemented by others on short term lease when required.

Berlin European UK   *United Kingdom*
A 737-300 (G-EURP) was delivered in October 1988 but immediately leased to Monarch. A second example (G-EURR) was delivered in April 1990 to begin IT charter work for the German travel industry. Another should be in service in 1991.

Braathens   *Norway*
The airline has been associated with the 737 since 1971 when its first Series 200 was delivered. Since then the type has been used on both domestic passenger schedules and IT work, the latter regularly taking the aircraft from Norway to the Mediterranean and Canary Islands. Braathens became a launch customer for the Series 500 with deliveries starting in 1990, joining the four -400s and those -200s not released by the arrival of the newcomers.

Left:
Braathens has possessed a number of 737-200s through the years, one of the older examples being LN-SUD. *AJW*

Braniff   *USA*
In September 1989 Braniff was once again in financial trouble and was forced to drastically reduce its network and fleet size. Ten 737-200s were retained for use on some of the remaining services, but the proposal to lease a large number of Series -200s and -300s from American Airlines in 1990 was suspended.

Brazilian Air Force   *Brazil*
Two 737-200s were delivered to the Brazilian Air Force in March and April 1976 for general transport and VIP duties with the identities FAB2115/6.

Britannia Airways   *United Kingdom*
Britannia chose the 737-200 for its future fleet and became the first European airline to put the type into service in 1968. Through the years the type has proved to be ideal for the extensive IT work carried out by the carrier, resulting in 29 being on strength at one point, supported by another five on lease. While the numbers of Series 200s are now declining due to the introduction of the 767 and the integration of seven ex-Orion Series 300s, the variant seems set to serve the airline for some years to come.

British Airways   *United Kingdom*
After some years of political opposition, British Airways finally ordered the 737-200 in the late 1970s. Intended for use on the carrier's shorter European routes, deliveries began in February 1980 with G-BGDC the forerunner of 19. A further batch of 16 began to arrive in 1984, with completion during the following year. In addition another nine were allocated to Airtours, but some were transferred from time to time to the parent company. After the take-over of British Caledonian in 1988 the charter subsidiary became Caledonian Airways, with an allocation of four 737s. However, these only remained until the end of the year when they became permanent members of the main fleet. Other 737s have been leased in, including four Series 300s from Maersk, the first of this variant to see service with the flag carrier. In October 1991 BA will begin to receive deliveries of the 24 aircraft on order for which the registration batch G-DOCA/Z has been reserved. Options are held on a further 11 and BA can specify which version it requires nearer the date.

British Airtours   *United Kingdom*
The 737-200 was chosen as the replacement type for the ageing 707s which had been used for some years by the British Airways charter subsidiary. Nine (G-BGJE/M) were allocated to the airline, with deliveries starting in March 1980. Nevertheless most spent time with BA when the latter was in need of capacity, and this resulted in Airtours leasing 737s in from Air Europe. From 1 April 1988 the airline began operating as Caledonian Airways.

British Midland   *United Kingdom*
In 1987 British Midland became a 737 operator for the first time when it introduced the Series 300 on to the Edinburgh service on 1 December. As the trunk routes expanded so additional 737s were introduced to bring the total of -300s to six (G-OBMA-D, H/J), plus a pair of the larger Series 400 (G-OBMF/G). During the summer of 1990 a third example of the latter (G-BOPJ) was acquired from Novair.

Busy Bee   *Norway*
As a subsidiary of Braathens, Busy Bee's sole 737-200 (LN-NPB) has frequently substituted for one of the parent company's aircraft since it was delivered in December 1979. At other times the aircraft is used for IT flights by Norwegian tour operators.

CAAC   *China*
After reorganisation of the airline industry in China, the CAAC was split up into regional carriers responsible for services within their own areas. China did not acquire any 737s until 1983 when the first of 16 Series 200s was delivered. This batch was quickly followed by eight -300s in 1985 which were promptly taken over by the new Yunnan Provincial and China Southwest Airlines. Together with Xiamen Airlines, the latter also received some of the earlier machines.

Caledonian Airways   *United Kingdom*
Caledonian formally took over the charter activities of Airtours and British Caledonian on 1 April 1988. It received four 737-200s (G-BGJF-I) for the first season but these were returned to BA before the end of the year. Leased examples were then used as an interim measure while awaiting delivery of its intended 757s, at which point the airline ceased its 737 operations.

Cameroon Airlines   *Cameroon*
Two 737-200s were acquired in 1972 to maintain a network of scheduled services within Africa. A third (TJ-CBD) was delivered in 1977, but its career was ended somewhat prematurely by a bomb at Doula, Cameroon, in August 1984. One year later its replacement became TJ-CBE to restore the fleet to a total of three Series 200.

Canadian Airlines International   *Canada*
This carrier came into being in January 1988 as a result of a merger between Pacific Western and

Above:
Although this 737-200 was given the identity CF-EPR when new with Eastern Provincial in December 1969, it has continued to carry it despite being absorbed in turn by Canadian Pacific and Canadian Airlines International. *G. W. Pennick*

Canadian Pacific, the latter having only recently reverted to this title after some years as CP Air. Both participants in the agreement had previously acquired other operators, many of which possessed a number of 737s. As a result, CAI inherited over 70 specimens of varied origins for use on the company's regional and domestic sectors. In addition, three -300s usually spend the winter in Canada on lease from Monarch.

China Airlines   *China*
A number of 737-200s have passed through the airline's hands but the current four in the fleet were delivered between 1986 and 1988. The type is used mainly for domestic services in Taiwan.

Condor   *West Germany*
Since its take-over by Lufthansa in 1959, Condor has operated charters and IT flights for its parent. After some years with 737-200s, the airline received the first of a batch of seven Series 300s in 1987 for use on the frequent excursions to the holiday areas on behalf of German tour operators. Some of Condor's 737s are operated by Sudflug and DFD, both of which are subsidiary companies.

Continental Airlines   *USA*
After virtually ceasing operations in 1983, Continental has emerged to become America's fourth largest airline. This was achieved by a series of take-overs including such 737 operators as People Express, Frontier and New York Air. Almost 100 assorted examples were therefore acquired including 17 Series 100s retired by Lufthansa in 1981 and sold to People Express for its proposed high frequency schedules.

COPA Panama   *Panama*
Two 737s are used by the carrier to maintain services to points in Central and South America plus the West Indies. One of the pair of airliners

(HP-873) is an ex-Singapore Series 100 of 1969 vintage while the second (HP-1134) is a Series 200 combi which served with Lufthansa as D-ABBE until joining Presidential Airways in 1985.

China Southwest Airlines   *China*
(*See* CAAC)

Corse Air   *France*
The carrier began replacing its Caravelle fleet in 1987 when the first 737-300 arrived on lease from GPA. In 1988 a second was obtained from the same source and together the pair carried out all Corse Air commitments for flying ITs to the Mediterranean and Canaries.

CP Air   *Canada*
(*See* Canadian Airlines International)

Cruzeiro do Sul   *Brazil*
Six 737-200s (PP-CJN-T) were delivered in 1975, and thereafter were used for the airline's domestic schedules.

Dan-Air   *United Kingdom*
Always an airline with a variety of types in its fleet, Dan-Air acquired its first 737-200 in 1980. During the decade several were leased for short-term stays, while others continued in the company's employ for IT work. A Series 300 (G-SCUH) was delivered in May 1985, with a second appearing in February 1988. Two Series 400s were added during 1988/89, with another of this variant expected in 1990.

Delta Airlines   *USA*
Following the take-over of Western Airlines in April 1987, Delta became the third largest carrier in the US. Already a keen collector of 737s, the merger also contributed another large batch to the formidable fleet of Series 200s. It also meant that the airline acquired its first Series 300s because Western already possessed 13 of the variant. Starting in 1993, Delta will take delivery of 50 additional 737s which will probably be a mix of Series 300s, 400s and 500s.

DETA Mozambique   *Mozambique*
Domestic and regional services have been operated by the three 737-200s in the fleet (C9-BAA, -BAC and -BAD) since they were delivered in the mid-1970s. In 1980 the airline adopted the new title of Linhas Aéreas de Mocambique (LAM).

DFD   *West Germany*
(*See* Condor)

Dragonair   *Hong Kong*
The airline was established in 1985 to offer scheduled and charter flights from Hong Kong. Some routes into China were started using three

737-200s, but it was denied access to many of the sectors requested. In 1990 an arrangement with Cathay Pacific should improve Dragonair's position considerably.

Eastern Provincial   *Canada*
(*See* Canadian Airlines International)

Eagle Air   *Iceland*
Two 737-200s (TF-ISA and -VLT) are used for the airline's international services from Reykjavik to Amsterdam, Hamburg, Milan and Zurich.

EgyptAir   *Egypt*
Seven 737-200s have been used since the mid-1970s to provide scheduled services between Cairo, the Middle East and Africa.

El Al   *Israel*
(*See* Arkia)

Ethiopean Airlines   *Ethiopia*
The first of two 737-200s was delivered to the airline in October 1987, its companion arriving in July 1988. Intended for some of the regional routes, the pair only worked together for two months before ET-AJA crashed in September leaving -AJB to continue alone.

Euralair   *France*
Inclusive tour charter flights are flown by the carrier's five 737-200s, many on behalf of Air Charter International. Three Series 500s are on order for delivery in 1991/92.

Europe Aero Service   *France*
Mainly an IT carrier, EAS also operates some of its aircraft for Air Charter. It has three 737-200s on strength, with one Series 300 joining them in 1989.

EuroBerlin France   *France*
Air France and Lufthansa combined forces to set up this scheduled service airline in the autumn of 1988. Monarch was contracted to provide the four 737-300s required, together with the necessary support, leading to operations starting in November with G-MONH, -MONL, -MONM and -MONN.

Far East Air Transport   *Taiwan*
Scheduled domestic services are flown with the help of six 737-200s and two -100s, the latter originally a part of the pioneering Lufthansa fleet at the end of 1967. The routes offered link Taipei with Hualien, Tainan, Makung and Kaosiung.

Faucett   *Peru*
Domestic schedules are covered by the carrier's one 737-100 and two -200s, although one of the latter (OB-1314, ex-El-ASB with Aer Lingus) was severely damaged in April 1989.

Above:
Federal Express took delivery of its first 737-200, N201FE in 1979. *Boeing*

Federal Express   *USA*
When permission to use larger capacity aircraft for the nightly parcel runs was received, Federal Express acquired five 737-200s (N201FE, N203FE-6FE). Delivered in 1979, a decision to standardise on the larger 727 meant that the twin jets had left the fleet by the end of 1981.

Finnair   *Finland*
(*See* Atlanta Icelandic)

Frontier   *USA*
From the early 1970s Frontier collected a variety of 737-200s to serve its extensive network, which spread from Canada to Mexico and from Illinois in the east to the Pacific coast. During 1985 the carrier and its 51 737s were taken over by People Express, itself absorbed by Continental one year later.

Futura   *Spain*
Aer Lingus has an interest in this latest airline wishing for a share in the IT market. Based at Palma, operations started in March 1990 using the Series 400 EC-ETB. Two more were due during the summer.

Garuda   *Indonesia*
The first (PK-GWA) of a batch of eight 737-300s was delivered to the airline in April 1989, with the remaining aircraft (PK-GWD-J) due to arrive at intervals to December 1990.

GB Airways   *Gibraltar*
Scheduled services are operated from Gatwick to North Africa and Gibraltar in addition to others from the latter base. Various 737-200s have been leased from both Air Europe and British Airways, but the appropriately registered specimens G-IBTY and -IBTZ were earmarked for the growing carrier in 1990.

Germania   *West Germany*
When formed in 1978 the airline was known as Special Air Transport but was renamed in June

1986. Re-equipment plans saw the retirement of the Caravelle fleet and the arrival of new 737-300s. Six of the latter were acquired in 1987/88 for use on the carrier's German IT charter flights, although two aircraft were later transferred to the Condor subsidiary, DFD, and one to Monarch as G-EURP.

Gulf Air   *Oman*
Eight 737-200s (A40-BC-BJ) were obtained in the late 1970s to operate on the carrier's routes to neighbouring Middle East countries.

Hapag-Lloyd   *West Germany*
This airline operates a wide range of IT charters from Germany to the Mediterranean, the Canaries and parts of Africa. It has been associated with the 737 since 1981, when the first Series 200s were delivered. These were joined by four -400s during 1989 while two more were expected during 1990. As the older machines are due for phasing out, they will be replaced by an equal number of Series 500s, with another pair following in 1991.

Hispania   *Spain*
Formed in 1983 after the collapse of TAE, Hispania began IT charters from various airports in Europe to the holiday areas. In 1985, leased 737s began to replace the existing Caravelles, but during 1987 the first of the carrier's own Series 300s were delivered. Five were in service two years later, with another two in prospect, but before the fleet could be further enlarged the company collapsed in July 1989 to terminate the career of a popular airline.

Iberia   *Spain*
For many years Iberia has used DC-9s of various types for its short haul services, but three 737-300s were leased in 1988 following a shortage of capacity. All were due to have returned to their owner by the end of March 1990.

Icelandair   *Iceland*
In April 1989 Icelandair began its re-equipment programme when it took delivery of the first of three 737-400s to replace its 727s on the European schedules.

ICS Inter Ciel Service   *France*
(*See* Intercargo Services)

Indian Air Force   *India*
All four of the 737-200s used by the military started their careers with Indian Airlines, although both VT-EFL/M were leased and subsequently returned to the airline after service as K2371/0. The other two were originally registered VT-EHW/X when in civil use, but became K2412/3 when bought by the military.

Indian Airlines   *India*
In order to maintain its considerable network of domestic and regional routes, through the years since the first was delivered in 1970, Indian Airlines has assembled a 30-strong fleet of 737-200s, six of which are leased from Transavia and GPA.

Indonesian Air Force   *Indonesia*
The 737-200 was used as the basis for a maritime version known as the Surveiller. Three were bought by the Indonesian Air Force (AI-7301/3) and could either be used as passenger transports or for their intended purpose.

Intercargo Service   *France*
Most of the airline's activities are concerned with the movement of mail and parcels at night for which purpose four 737-200s are on strength. They are also operated on an occasional basis for Air Charter International in a 130-seat passenger mode. Recently the airline changed its name to ICS Inter Ciel Service.

Inter European   *United Kingdom*
This carrier was launched by Aspro Holidays in 1986 with IT charter operations commencing the

Below:
Hispania leased several 737-200s to replace its Caravelles in the mid-1980s. This example was Transavia's PH-TVS before adopting EC-DVN as its identity. *AJW*

following year with leased 737-200s. These were replaced with the delivery of new Series 300s (G-BNGL/M) leased from GPA in the spring of 1988, while a third (G-IEAA) was added in the late summer of 1989.

Iranair   *Iran*
Three 737-200s were acquired in the early 1970s and have subsequently been employed on domestic and regional services. A fourth specimen (EP-AGA) is configured with a VIP interior and used by the government since 1977.

Iran Government   *Iran*
(*See* Iranair)

Iraqi Airways   *Iraq*
Two 737-200 combis were delivered to the airline in 1974, and are generally employed on some of the domestic and regional routes.

Istanbul Airlines   *Turkey*
Originally only a charter airline, in December 1989 a scheduled service to Munich begun. Authority is also held for the Hamburg and Cologne routes which will be launched in conjunction with the delivery of the airline's second 737.

Jugoslav Airlines (JAT)   *Yugoslavia*
Until 1985 JAT relied upon 727s and DC-9s for its scheduled services, but during the year the first of nine 737-300s was delivered, and these are now to be seen at most European airports.

KLM   *Netherlands*
The Dutch flag carrier has always been a supporter of Douglas products, but for its DC-9 replacement it chose the 737-300. Deliveries started in 1986 with PH-BDA, followed by another 12 aircraft during the next three years or so. In addition several Series 200s and 300s were leased from Transavia until the batch was completed. KLM's fleet was further increased by three -400s (PH-BDR-T) in 1989, which were due to be joined by four more of the species in the next year.

Kuwait Airways   *Kuwait*
One 737-200 (9K-ACV) was delivered to the company in 1976 for use on its regional schedules, but after more than four years of lone service the machine was sold in favour of the larger 727, thereby ending the carrier's association with the twin jet.

LADECO   *Chile*
During the first three years of the 1980s LADECO received three 737-200s. These entered service on the carrier's international and domestic sectors, but after a fairly short time it was decided to standardise on the 727. By 1986 all the twin jets had been sold.

Above:
JAT began assembling its 737-300 fleet in 1985 with YU-AND. *A. S. Wright*

LAN Chile   *Chile*
A number of 737-200s have been used by the airline, although the majority have been leased from GPA. Four were in service in 1989 to cover the domestic and regional routes operated from Santiago.

Lauda Air   *Austria*
In 1985 Lauda Air leased a 737-200 from Transavia for use on IT flights to the Mediterranean and the Canaries. Registered OE-ILE, the machine was finally returned upon the arrival of the airline's second Series 300 (OE-ILG); the first having been delivered in 1986 as OE-ILF. Lauda is due to receive a third -300 in 1991.

Lina Congo   *Congo*
When Air Liberia released its sole 737 in 1982 it was acquired by Lina Congo for its growing international routes. Registered TN-AEE, the combi has remained the carrier's sole example.

Linhas Aéreas de Mocambique (LAM)   *Mozambique*
(*See* DETA Mozambique)

Linjeflyg   *Sweden*
Although for many years one of Fokker's best customers for the F-28, in 1989 the airline decided that the 737-500 was well suited to its requirements. Eight of the type were therefore ordered, with deliveries spread between 1990 and 1992. They will be used on the extensive domestic route network in addition to IT work.

Lufthansa   *West Germany*
As launch customer for the 737 in the 1960s, Lufthansa received its first aircraft at the end of 1967. This batch of Series 100s remained with the carrier until the early 1980s when they were sold to People Express and Far East Air Transport. Subsequently the airline has employed numerous -200s on most of its short-haul European sectors,

Above:
Lufthansa has included the 737-300 in its fleet since the mid-1980s. *AJW*

which in 1986 also saw the first of 23 Series 300s ordered by the German carrier. Steps were also taken to prepare for the eventual replacement of the earlier model by ordering 34 Series 500s, the first of which was scheduled to appear in October 1990.

Luxair   *Luxembourg*
Two 737-200s (LX-LGH/I) joined Luxair in 1977/78, and were subsequently used for IT charter work to the holiday areas and the longer scheduled routes from Luxembourg. In 1988 a third (LX-LGN) was leased from Sabena.

Maersk Air   *Denmark*
Through the years Maersk has possessed a number of 737s, starting with OY-APG in 1976. Although the airline uses the type for IT charters on behalf of Danish tour operators, for much of the time they are leased to other carriers around the world. With the advent of the Series 300, Maersk adopted this version for its activities; 10 being delivered by the end of 1989. Similarly the -500 will take over from the remaining -200s when the four on order are delivered in the early 1990s.

Malaysian Airlines   *Malaysia*
The 737-200s have been used for the airline's domestic and some regional services since the first was delivered in 1972. From 1990 some of the duties were due to become the responsibility of the Series 400 and later the -500, for which orders for 10 and six respectively have been placed with Boeing.

Malev   *Hungary*
Towards the end of 1988 Malev took the unusual step of leasing three 737-200s (HA-LEA-C) from GPA instead of using the customary Russian source. They entered service on some of the airline's European scheduled services.

Markair   *USA*
Formerly Alaska International Air, the carrier adopted its present name in 1984 to coincide with the receipt of five 737-200 combis. These are used for intrastate schedules together with passenger charters, while some services are operated for Alaskan Airlines.

Mexican Air Force   *Mexico*
When the first 737 joined the Mexican Air Force in 1980 it was after 11 years service with Western Air Lines. Initially it was identified as TP-03, but after three months this was changed to B-12001. Barely had the paint dried than it reverted to TP-03, but again it was only a short time before the signwriter was applying 12001, its present serial. It is used as a VIP transport for the government. The second machine was a Series 100 which duly received the identity TP-04, but eventually it was demobbed to become a corporate transport.

Mey-Air   *Norway*
This airline was formed in 1970 to undertake passenger charters and IT services from Oslo. For this purpose two 737-200s (LN-MTC/D) were delivered in October 1971, but unfortunately the company was forced to cease its activities in February 1974 when declared bankrupt. Both aircraft were repossessed by Boeing in early March and resold to Piedmont.

Midway   *USA*
Operations were started in November 1979, and the airline now has a network serving 54 airports along the east coast from Boston to Florida. A number of these destinations were added when Air Florida was absorbed in 1984, at the same time acquiring additional 737s. The type is still used, although the carrier has now adopted the MD87 for future expansion.

Monarch Airlines   *United Kingdom*

The first 737-200s were introduced in 1980 at a time when the 720s were nearing retirement. Thereafter more of the type operated the company's numerous IT charters until phased out in favour of Series 300s by 1988. Monarch also operates four of this variant for EuroBerlin France.

NASA   *USA*

The original 737 prototype was sold to NASA in July 1973 after concluding its development work with Boeing. Re-registered N515NA, its new owner has used it for a variety of test programmes including those involved with the new generation avionics.

New York Air   *USA*

This subsidiary of Texas Air began low-cost, high-frequency services between New York and Washington in December 1980. The network quickly spread southwards, and with it came the customary rapid growth in fleet size. The first of its new 737-300s arrived in August 1985, with subsequent deliveries taking the total to six by the end of the year. More followed in 1986, but sadly the parent company decided to merge New York Air with another of its possessions, Continental Airlines. So on 1 February 1987 the distinctive red livery began to disappear.

New Zealand National Airways
New Zealand

(*See* Air New Zealand)

Nihon Kinyori Airways   *Japan*

One of Japan's two regional airlines, Nihon Kinyori was formed in 1974. A 737-200 (JA8413) was bought from All Nippon in 1983 to be used on the longer sectors not suitable for the YS-11s in the fleet. In April 1987 the airline was renamed Air Nippon, and a second 737 (JA8415) joined the company in 1988.

Niger Government   *Niger*

One 737-200 (5U-BAG) was bought by the Government of Niger in 1978 for general transport duties, a role in which it has since continued.

Nigeria Airways   *Nigeria*

Two new 737-200s joined the airline in 1973 for use on some of the domestic and regional services. At the time a collection of Friendships and Fellowships carried out this work, but by the end of the decade these were being phased out in favour of more 737s. Five Irish-registered specimens were leased from GPA until the airline's own order for six was fulfilled in 1982.

Nordair   *Canada*

(*See* Canadian Airlines International)

Northwest Territorial Airways (NWT Air)
Canada

In addition to its cargo work, NWT Air operates passenger services in northern Canada with a pair of 737-200s leased from American Airlines. Schedules are also flown on behalf of Air Canada, to which it is affiliated.

Nortjet   *Spain*

This is but one of a number of Spanish airlines which were created in the late 1980s to win a share of the IT market from foreign carriers. From the start of operations in 1989 Nortjet has operated 737-400s from its Palma base, three being leased from GPA as EC-EMI, -EMY and -EPN.

Norway Airlines   *Norway*

Formed in 1987 to operate ITs from its home country, the airline's two 737-300s (LN-NOR/S) have nevertheless spent long periods on lease to UK carriers. In early 1989 it became a part of the Airlines of Europe Group, whereupon the name Air Europe Scandinavia was assumed, and the operation of schedules from Sweden, Norway and Denmark to Gatwick began for fellow group member, Air Europe.

Novair International   *United Kingdom*

Until 1989 the airline flew its numerous IT charters using three DC-10-10s, but in March and April two 170-seat 737-400s (G-BOPJ/K) were delivered to assist in the task. Unfortunately they arrived at a point when capacity was not needed due to the rapid decline in leisure travel, so in early 1990 both were offered for sale. Efforts similarly to dispose of the company were unsuccessful, which led to the decision to close down the operation on 5 May. A third -400 ordered for 1991 delivery, as well as two 1992 options were also sold.

Olympic Airways   *Greece*

Following a period of reorganisation in 1975, the airline acquired the 737-200 for use on its European schedules. The first four arrived in 1976, with a larger batch in 1980/81 taking the total to 11.

Orion Airways   *United Kingdom*

The East Midlands-based Orion began commercial work in March 1980 by flying IT passengers to the various holiday areas. Three 737-200s (G-BGTV, -BGTW and -BGTY) constituted the fleet for the first season but another three (G-BHVH-J) were added in 1981. Each year the total increased until a peak was reached in 1984, with 11 Series 200s in use. Orion became the first European operator of the Series 300 in 1985, which then allowed a steady reduction in the number of the earlier version. Scheduled services were begun

Above:
Two Britannia 737-200s wait alongside a Caledonian specimen and the Orion Series 300 G-BLKC. A Dan-Air 727 keeps them company. *AJW*

on five routes in 1986, while operations were expanded at other airports such as Gatwick, Manchester and Glasgow. Sadly during 1988 negotiations were completed for the sale of the carrier to the Thomson Group which meant that the aircraft were absorbed by Britannia during 1989.

Pacific Southwest   USA
In the late 1960s PSA began to assemble a fleet of 737-200s for use on its high-density, high-frequency schedules in California. After receiving 11 of the type, the airline opted for a combination of DC-9s and 727s instead, so by 1975 all the 737s had been sold to other carriers.

Pacific Western   Canada
(*See* Canadian Airlines International)

Pakistan International Airlines   Pakistan
PIA took delivery of its entire 737-300 fleet in June 1985, the six aircraft (AP-BCA-F) taking over some of the busier domestic sectors in addition to a number of regional routes.

Pan Am   USA
A number of 737-200s were leased by Pan Am in 1983 for service on the company's German network. With the delivery of new A310s and the return of 727s to Europe, the 737s were gradually transferred back to the US. Five remained in use on the carrier's East Coast services in 1989.

People Express   USA
(*See* Continental Airlines)

Philippine Airlines   Philippines
The airline began to take delivery of 10 Irish registered 737-300s during 1989 after the type was chosen for use on the extensive scheduled network. All of the aircraft were leased from GPA, but subsequently one (EI-BZG) was written off at Manila following an explosion on 11 May 1990.

Piedmont   USA
(*See* USAir)

Pluna   Uruguay
Three 737-200s were delivered to the airline in 1982 for use on its international schedules linking Montevideo with other South American centres. During a number of summer periods in the 1980s, one of the aircraft found its way to Europe for lease to Transavia and on some occasions temporary service with Britannia.

Polynesian Airlines   Western Samoa
Polynesian's association with the 737 has been restricted to 5W-PAL, which was delivered in 1981. Intended for use on the scheduled services linking Samoa with Auckland and Sydney, nevertheless it was leased out for several periods until finally leaving the company's employ in 1987.

Presidential Airways   USA
Washington (Dulles) became the base and operations hub of Presidential Airlines when it was formed in 1985. Most of the activities centre around the northeast of the US, operating as part of the Continental Express system. A number of elderly, secondhand 737-200s were acquired initially, but in 1987 most had been replaced by new BAe146s and Jetstreams. Financially troubled in mid-1989, Presidential ceased operations in December.

Quebecair   Canada
(*See* Canadian Airlines International)

Rotterdam Airlines   Netherlands
Ambitious plans were made by Rotterdam Airlines in the early 1980s, which included a number of scheduled services from its home base. Although a 737-200 (PH-RAL) was leased from Trans European in anticipation, financial support was not forthcoming so the airline's career was short and non-operational.

Below:
Polynesian's 737-200 5W-PAL was avoiding a thunderstorm when seen on a test flight in 1981. *Boeing*

Royal Air Maroc   *Morocco*
The airline's first 737-200s were delivered in 1975, but it was 1982/83 before the fleet was further expanded. All have been used on the airline's network, which includes routes between Casablanca, North and West Africa, Europe and other Moroccan centres. The carrier opted for the Series 400 when seeking greater capacity, two of the variant being ordered for delivery in 1990.

Royal Brunei Airlines   *Brunei*
Since 1975 the airline has employed several 737-200s on the frequent services linking the capital with neighbouring centres such as Bangkok, Darwin, Kuala Lumpur, Manila and Singapore.

Royal Swazi   *Swaziland*
Between October 1982 and November 1983 the airline possessed one 737-200 (3D-ADA), which was used for its schedules to South Africa and other neighbouring countries.

Royal Thai Air Force   *Thailand*
A 737-200 was delivered to the Royal Thai Air Force in 1983 and given the serial 22-222 for services with the Royal Flight. The latter also received a Series 300 in 1989, which was allocated 33-333 as its identity.

Sabena   *Belgium*
Since taking delivery of its first 737-200 in 1974 the Belgian flag carrier has used the type extensively on its European route network. In 1987 four Series 300s were received, with two more arriving two years later.

SAHSA   *Honduras*
Several 737-200s have been operated by the airline through the years, principally to link Honduras with Central and North American centres.

Saudia   *Saudi Arabia*
In the early 1970s many of the domestic routes were serviced by DC-3s, but in 1972 a programme of replacement was begun, whereupon the first of an eventually large fleet of 737-200s arrived. The type is also operated on international services from Jeddah.

Sobelair   *Belgium*
Mainly an IT charter operator, Sobelair has possessed a number of 737-200s to carry out these commitments, although frequently they have been leased to other carriers. Since it is closely associated with Sabena, replacements are normally transferred as required. Sobelair took delivery of its first Series 300 (OO-SBZ) in mid-1987.

South African Airways   *South Africa*
The airline was an early customer for the 737-200, and has continued to employ the type on its extensive domestic and regional routes since the first aircraft was delivered in 1968.

South Korean Airlines   *South Korea*
In 1985 a new 737-300 (85101) was delivered to the air force to operate as a VIP transport on behalf of the government.

Southwest Airlines   *USA*
Coincident with a change of title, the newly created Dallas-based Southwest Airlines began operations in 1971 with three 737-200s. As the network of high-frequency, low-cost services increased, so did the fleet expand. The airline's apparently insatiable appetite for the type resulted in 48 Series 300s joining the 46 older specimens by the end of 1989, with another dozen in prospect for the early 1990s. Southwest also became a launch customer for the -500, bringing the company the distinction of becoming the first to take delivery of the variant at the end of February 1990.

Southwest Airlines Japan   *Japan*
The Japanese regional airline operates scheduled services which include seven 737-200s. Southwest is a subsidiary of Japan Air Lines and commenced operations in July 1967.

Spantax   *Spain*
This carrier concentrated its activities on passenger IT charters to and from its Palma base for almost 30 years after its launch in 1959. During 1984 the need to replace its elderly Cv990 fleet was responsible for the arrival of a number of 737-200s on lease from a variety of sources. In 1987 the MD83 series was chosen as a permanent solution so the 737s returned to the lessors. They therefore missed the airline's demise in March, 1988, that brought an end to an unusually long career.

Sudan Airways   *Sudan*
Two 737-200s (ST-AFK/L) have been used by Sudan Airways since 1975 for its regional services to such places as Cairo and Jeddah.

Sudflug   *West Germany*
See Condor.

Sultan Air   *Turkey*
Charters were begun in August 1988 using a pair of Caravelles leased from Transwede. The same source supplied a pair of 737-200s in 1990 (SE-DKG/H) both originating from the Braathens fleet.

Sunexpress   *Turkey*
Another of the batch of new Turkish carriers,

Sunexpress is associated with Lufthansa and THY. It was expected to begin IT work during 1990 with one 737-300 registered TC-SUN. Another two aircraft are anticipated for service in 1991.

Sunworld International Airways   *USA*
Although basically a DC-9 operator, Sunworld leased a total of four 737-300s between 1985 and 1987 to assist on the company's scheduled service activities along the US West Coast. All of this came to an abrupt stop in November 1988 when the carrier ended its operations.

Supair   *West Germany*
Holiday charter flights from Munich were planned by this new carrier in late 1980. As an interim measure a 737-200 was leased from Maersk as D-ADDA, but its stay in Germany was short. With no authority to start up, Supair's prospects were not encouraging so the aircraft was quickly returned to Denmark. Two new 737s ordered from Boeing were never built, although the identities D-ADDB/C were reserved.

TAAG Angola Airlines   *Angola*
In 1975 TAAG began to re-equip with 737-200s for use on its international routes in Africa. Subsequently the airline has operated a total of 10 different specimens, two of which were leased for a period in 1981. Of the remainder three were destroyed in various mishaps in 1980, 1983 and 1984 to leave five currently in service.

TACA International   *El Salvador*
One 737-200 (YS-O8C) was bought in 1978 for use on the carrier's international routes to Central and North America until 1985 when the aircraft was sold. In the meantime other examples of the model were leased in the 1980s, plus a Series 300 in 1988, but all have retained their US identities.

TAME   *Ecuador*
The country's principal domestic carrier took delivery of 737-200 HC-BIG in 1981, but almost two years later it crashed and was not replaced.

TEA Basle   *Switzerland*
This Swiss-based member of the TEA Group was formed in 1988 to fly IT charters to the Mediterranean and Canary Islands with two 737-300s (HB-IIA/B).

TEA France   *France*
Operations began in October 1989 when this latest TEA Group airline was licensed to fly IT charters from Lille and Lourdes to the Mediterranean holiday areas. Two 737-300s (F-GKTA/B) were transferred from the Belgian parent company.

TEA UK   *United Kingdom*
Trans European acquired Mediterranean Express after the latter's demise, so that it could be re-established at Birmingham as the first of the TEA Group of carriers. Renamed TEA UK, it was equipped with three 737-200s (G-BTEB, -BTEC and -BTED) to enable IT charter work to commence while awaiting the delivery of the intended -300s. The first of the latter (G-TEAB) arrived in March 1990.

Thai Airways   *Thailand*
The three 737-200s in the airline's fleet are used for the busier domestic sectors and some of the regional operations. Re-equipment plans include the introduction of seven Series 400s between 1990 and 1993.

Transair Canada   *Canada*
Four 737-200s were used by this Canadian domestic operator in the 1970s. In 1979 the airline became a part of Pacific Western and the aircraft were absorbed into the latter's fleet. They had been sold by the time Canadian Pacific took over in 1987.

Below:
Based at Birmingham, 737-200 G-BTEC was one of three flown by TEA (UK) when operations started in 1989. *AJW*

Transavia   *Netherlands*

Although the airline operates one scheduled service between Amsterdam and Gatwick with a 737, most of its activities concern IT charters and leasing of its aircraft to other carriers. Both Series 200s and -300s are employed for all purposes, with others being leased in from time to time to cover any shortage of capacity.

Transbrazil   *Brazil*

Prior to 1986 Transbrazil had not operated any 737s, but during the year deliveries of 11 leased Series 300s began. Three -400s were also received during 1989, in this case leased from GPA.

Trans European Airways   *Belgium*

Since its formation in 1970, TEA has concentrated on IT charters and the lease of its aircraft to other operators. In 1988 it expanded by setting up a group of carriers in other European countries, all equipped with 737-300s transferred from the

parent. This expansion is expected to continue with the delivery of additional examples of the type.

Transmed   *Egypt*

Formed to undertake charter services from Cairo, operations began in December 1989 with a 737-200 (G-BGYJ) leased from Britannia. Upon its return to its owner the aircraft was due to be replaced with another pair of the species from a different source.

Transwede   *Sweden*

Passenger charters are flown from Scandinavia to all parts of Europe. In 1989 two 737-200s were leased (SE-DKG/H) for sub-lease to Sultan Air, while later in the year a pair of Series 300s (SE-DLN/O) were received to complement the MD83 fleet.

Tunis Air   *Tunisia*

Two 737-200s were delivered in each of 1979 and 1981, from which date the type has been used on most of the airline's international routes to European centres. Two Series 500s are on order for 1992/93 delvery.

UAE Government   *Emirates*

Two 737-200s (A6-AAA and A6-ESH) with VIP interiors are operated by the governments of Abu Dhabi and Sharjah for the use of the Royal Flight.

United Airlines   *USA*

As one of the original customers for the 737-200, through the years United increased the number it had in service to over 70 by acquiring 25 secondhand examples from Frontier in 1985. Deliveries of Series 300s began in November 1986, with the total in service reaching three figures by 1990. Repeat orders will further increase the number, although an option is held so that the -500 can be substituted if required.

Universair   *Spain*

Charter operations were started by this new Palma-based carrier in 1987 using a pair of leased 737-300s (EC-EDM and EC-EGQ), joined in 1988 by a third (EC-EID). Future plans include the arrival of another two 737s, but depending upon demand.

USAir   *USA*

The airline's first 737 was delivered in 1982, with 23 being in service two years later. This total was greatly increased following the integration of Piedmont's 62 aircraft in 1987. Two years earlier both carriers had begun to accept the new Series 300s, so an impressive number of this variant also found themselves united in a common livery. After the merger USAir began to take delivery of its -400s and these are expected to continue to arrive well in to the 1990s.

USAF   *USA*

In need of a navigation trainer without the expense of initiating a new design, the USAF ordered 19 737-200s for delivery in 1973/74. For this purpose the modified variant was designated T-43A.

Vacationair   *Canada*

Newly formed in 1987, the Toronto-based charter carrier acquired two 737-200s to fly passengers to the holiday areas of the US. Vacationair also found the need for others on short-term leases to assist in the busy winter period, but in December 1989 the airline experienced financial problems and operations ceased.

Varig   *Brazil*

A wide range of domestic services are flown by Varig's 737s, the first of which was delivered in 1974. With a total of 12 Series 200s in the fleet, in 1987 the carrier changed to the -300 for the next nine additions.

VASP   *Brazil*

A large, assorted collection of 737-200s are operated on the carrier's services which link all parts of Brazil. These were augmented in 1987 by six Series 300s leased from GPA.

Venezuelan Air Force   *Venezuela*

The serial FAV0001 was allocated to the 737-200 bought by the government in October 1976. It is equipped with a VIP interior.

Viva Air   *Spain*

This Palma-based carrier chose the 737-300 for its fleet requirements when it was formed in 1988. Five were in use for the airline's IT charter flights during 1989 and another four were in the offing for future leases in 1991 and 1992.

Western Airlines   *USA*
(*See* Delta Airlines)

Wien Air Alaska   *USA*

A extensive network of scheduled services were operated throughout Alaska and down the US West Coast. A fleet of 10 737-200s was built up in the 1970s and early 1980s, but in 1984 the airline changed its name to Wien Airlines and reduced the fleet size to three aircraft. In October 1985 the carrier ceased operations and was declared bankrupt.

Wien Airlines   *USA*
(*See* Wien Air Alaska)

Xiamen Airlines   *China*
(*See* CAAC)

Zambia Airways   *Zambia*

A single 737-200 (9J-AEG) has served with the airline since new in 1976. While not overworked, it includes both domestic and international routes to other African states in its programme of activities.

Below:
This Series 300 operated by Viva Air is clearly showing the undercarriage retraction system common to all the 737 range.   *G. W. Pennick*